A Proclamation for Peace

Translated for the World

edited by
Allison deFreese
& Kim Stafford

in collaboration with the
Oregon Society of Translators
and Interpreters

Little Infinities
Portland, Oregon
2024

This book copyright © 2024 Allison deFreese & Kim Stafford. Translations & audio in this book copyright © 2024 by their translators and readers.

Print ISBN: 979-8-9910558-0-2
E-book: ISBN: 979-8-9910558-2-6
LCCN: 2024913421

"A Proclamation for Peace," by Kim Stafford, is reprinted from *Wild Honey, Tough Salt* by permission of Red Hen Press. Selected translations in this book first appeared in *World Literature Today*, *Eunoia Review*, and *Cathexis Northwest Press*. The Introduction is adapted from a note published in *World Literature Today*'s summer 2024 feature on this project. And thanks to Michael Nye for the cover photo (you can find information about this image at the end of the book).

Thanks to Ghada Mourad, Didier Chan Quijano, and Kathy Van de Vate who helped curate some of these translations. And thanks to Kata Beilin, Kunzang Choden, Ileana Marin, Krzysztof Czyżewski, Romina Espinosa, AKaiser, Paul E. Riek & Aurelia Sánchez López, and Steve Shankman, who referred translators and readers to us. Thanks to Sinéad Quirke Køngerskov who composed two translations, helped to edit the language notes, and took a devoted look at the entire manuscript. And thanks to Ali Shaw and Jenny Kimura at Indigo: Editing, Design, and More, for their assistance with book production.

As translation is an art, and though we made every effort to ensure the accuracy of translations in this book, the complexities of proofing world languages make perfect accuracy a challenge. With help, we may refine these texts in a second edition, and perhaps add others.

With deep gratitude to our translators across the world who brought this poem into their beautiful languages, this book is for the children.

سلام

խաղաղութիւն

grašak

pau

ཞི་བདེ

vrede

ཞྀད་དོང་ངོ་

paco

paix

síocháin

ειρήνη

Frieden

ειρήνη

thak

words for peace

שָׁלוֹם

béke

friður

pace

和平

amani

aşîtî

pax

pis

平和

शान्ति

fred

سوله

صلح

pokój

امن

wakin

śandipen

мир

la paz

kapayapan

அமைதி

สันติภาพ

barış

hòa bình

alafia

ets'a'an óolal

Introduction
by Allison deFreese

This project grew from a conversation with Kim Stafford during the Oregon Society of Translators and Interpreters conference, "Words = A Pathway to Peace." We sent a poem for peace around the planet by translating the former Oregon Poet Laureate's "A Proclamation for Peace" into world languages. There is much in this world we cannot change, but this was something we could, using the tools we had at hand: our words and our knowledge of many languages.

"Hope seems small, sometimes," Kim writes, while "kindness is seldom in the news and peace an abstraction." Yet, at a time when *the world is too much with us*, these translations are not an abstraction; they are a way to summon change by broadcasting a call for peace. The project has now become a global effort, with nearly every world region represented.

One joy in compiling these translations has been to observe how translators from diverse countries and cultures call for world peace using unique interpretations of Kim's words. In the French adaptation by Anne-Charlotte Giovangrandi, the proclamation becomes a *Déclaration de paix* (if we can "declare" war, why not peace?), while Tram Bui and Hai Tran see the poem as a "plea for peace" (lời khẩn cầu) in Vietnamese. Prabu Muruganantham signals peace with the drumbeat of a murasu (**அமைதிய**) in his Tamil translation.

The selections in this book surged from a democratic and organic process, with the translators often referring other translators to our cause. Early on, two very different Japanese translations arrived on the same day, and though the original goal was to feature one translation per language, we chose to include both. Some translators who contributed to this project have published multiple books, won international awards, or are directors of graduate translation programs, while for others, "A Proclamation for Peace" marks their first translation or publication. And this is how it should be. A community needs wisdom and experience, yes, but also opens channels where new voices can grow and shine. Admittedly, neither Kim nor I are fluent in every language represented in this book, so editing the manuscript has required collaboration and trust. I am grateful to the translators who had their work reviewed by colleagues or volunteered as editors for other translations in this book.

For decades, the Stafford family has been "walking away" from war (as William Stafford wrote), while sowing peace through poetry. Yes, our lives may seem short in 2024. Yes, we may be afraid. Yet may our words and translations reach far for cross-cultural understanding and peace.

Contents

Introduction by Allison deFreese

- 6 English by Kim Stafford
- 8 Arabic by El Habib Louai
- 10 Armenian by Vardan Aslanyan
- 12 Ashaninka by Marilu Iroba Cipriani
- 14 Bislama by Bob Hazen & Marie-Therese Serveux
- 16 Bosnian by Adna Mehić
- 18 Bulgarian by Gabriela Manova & Rumen Pavlov
- 20 Catalan by AKaiser & Jaume C. Pons Alorda
- 22 Classical Tibetan/Choekey by Anonymous
- 24 Danish by Sinéad Quirke Køngerskov
- 26 Dutch by Dafne Dahle
- 28 Dzongkha by Anonymous
- 30 Esperanto by AKaiser
- 32 French by Anne-Charlotte Giovangrandi
- 34 Gaeilge by Sinéad Quirke Køngerskov
- 36 German by Malcolm Goldman
- 38 Greek by Konstantina Velisari
- 40 Hebrew by Robert Alter
- 42 Hungarian by Erika Kóródi
- 44 Icelandic by Kári Tulinius
- 46 Italian by Marella Feltrin-Morris
- 48 Japanese I by Mika Shimizu Jarmusz
- 50 Japanese II by Liu Jionghao
- 52 Kiswahili by Dunia Mirindi
- 54 Kurdish by Nasrin Mohammed
- 56 Latin by Simona Gauchers Mancini
- 58 Mandarin by Liu Jionghao

60 Nepali by Daya Shakya
62 Newar by Daya Shakya & Arun Shrestha
64 Norwegian by Bjarne Bjørnevik
66 Pashto by Zaher Wahab
68 Persian by Alireza Taghdarreh
70 Polish by Monika Pilecka
72 Portuguese by Scott McClain &
      Elizabeth Setti Esmay
74 Punjabi by Moazzam Sheikh & Amna Ali
76 Quechua by Guipsy Alata Ramos
78 Romani by Agnieszka Caban
80 Romanian by Ileana Marin
82 Russian by Gleb & Vita Sapozhnikov
84 Spanish (Latin American) by Romina Espinosa
86 Spanish (world) by D. P. Snyder
88 Swedish by Henrik Otterberg
90 Tagalog by Su Layug
92 Tamil by Prabu Muruganantham
94 Thai by Piyawee Ruenjinda & Jeta Jiranuntarat
96 Turkish by F. Gülşen Buecher
98 Ukrainian by Iana Ianovska
100 Upper Austrian by Carola F. Berger
102 Vietnamese by Tram Bui & Hai Tran
104 Yoruba by Abayomi Animashaun
106 Yucatec Maya by Lizbeth Carrillo Can
108 Zapotec by Fr. Eleazar López Hernández
111 Afterword by Kim Stafford
113 Notes on languages, audio, & cover photo

English

Original poem by Kim Stafford

Kim Stafford is a writer who teaches and travels to raise the human spirit. He founded the Northwest Writing Institute at Lewis & Clark College in 1986, and is the author of some twenty books of poetry and prose. He served as Oregon Poet Laureate 2018-2020, and has taught writing in Scotland, Italy, Mexico, and Bhutan.

English read by Kim Stafford

A Proclamation for Peace

Whereas the world is a house on fire;
Whereas the nations are filled with shouting;
Whereas hope seems small, sometimes
   a single bird on a wire
   left by migration behind.

Whereas kindness is seldom in the news
   and peace an abstraction
   while war is real;

Whereas words are all I have;
Whereas my life is short;
Whereas I am afraid;
Whereas I am free—despite all
   fire and anger and fear;

Be it therefore resolved a song
shall be my calling—a song
not yet made shall be vocation
and peaceful words the work
of my remaining days.

Arabic

translated by El Habib Louai ترجمة الحبيب الواعي

El Habib Louai is a Moroccan poet, translator, musician, and assistant professor of English at Ibn Zohr University in Agadir, Morocco. His poetry, as well as his articles about and translations into Arabic of Beat writers, have appeared in many literary magazines and journals. Louai's Arabic translations include *America, America: An Anthology of Beat Poetry in Arabic*, Michael Rothenberg's collection of poems entitled *Indefinite Detention: A Dog Story*, Bob Kaufman's *The Ancient Rain*, Giorgio Agamben's *What is an Apparatus and Other Essays*, and Diane di Prima's *Revolutionary Letters*. Louai has published two collections of poems: *Mrs. Jones Will Now Know: Poems of a Desperate Rebel* and *Rotten Wounds Embalmed with Tar*, which was a finalist for the 2020 Sillerman First Book Prize for African Poetry.

Arabic read by El Habib Louai

نداء السلام

طالما أن العالم صار مسكنا تلتهمه النيران،
وطالما أن الأمم خنقها النحيب،
وصار الأمل ضئيلا، أحيانا محض طائر
وحيد فوق سلك معدني
خلفته الهجرة وراءها
وطالما أن الرأفة ندرت
والسلام أصبح تجريدا
في حين أن الحرب صارت حقيقة،
وطالما أن الكلمات هي كل ما أملك،
وطالما أن أيامي معدودة،
وطالما أنني خائف،
وطالما أنني حر —— رغم
النار والغضب والخوف،
فقد قررت أن تكون الأغنية
رسالتي —— أغنية
لم تبدع بعد ستكون دعوتي
وستكون الكلمات المطمئنة هاجس
ما تبقى من أيامي.

Armenian

translated by Vardan Aslanyan

Vardan Aslanyan, PhD/DD, is a deacon, translator, and Thoreauvian. He is a post-doc researcher at the University of Halle-Wittenberg in Germany.

Armenian read by Vardan Aslanyan

Ազդարարում հանուն խաղաղության

Մինչ աշխարհը հրդեհված մի տուն է,
Մինչ ազգերն ադադակով են լցվել,
Մինչ հույսը երբեմն չնչին է.
Չվիզ ետ մնացած, թվում է,
Մենակ թոչնակի պես լարին է թառել։
Մինչ լուրերում բարությունը սակավադեպ է,
Խաղաղությունը վերացություն է, իսկ
պատերազմն՝ իրական։
Մինչ իմ ունեցածը լոկ բառեր են,
Մինչ կյանքս կարճ է
Եվ վախն է տիրական։
Մինչդեռ ես ազատ եմ
Այս կրակին, գայրույթին ու վախին հակառակ,
Եղիցի ուրեմն երգն իմ կոչումը՝
Դեռևս չարարված մի երգի
Ու խաղաղաբեր բառերի ստեղծումը,
Մնացյալ օրերիս աշխատանքը համակ։

Ashaninka

translated by Marilu Iroba Cipriani, and reviewed by Deniz Fidel Contreras Alva

Marilu Iroba Cipriani is a teacher who trained as a translator and interpreter in the Satipo Ashaninka language at the Ministry of Culture in Peru. She is a certified evaluator of communicative language skills through Peru's *Sistema Nacional de Evaluación, Acreditación y Certificación de la Calidad Educativa*. She currently works for the Board of Indigenous Languages as an Ashaninka language interpretation and translation analyst.

Ashaninka read by Marilu Iroba Cipriani

Ikobabentajeitiro akametsatabakantsi

Añayetakero aipatsiteki bashinonkantsiyetantsi;
Añayebetakaro pashini
nampitsipe kantibentajeibetakarori
Ompiakonentabetaka kapichaji tera
yakakoyeteri, yaratakopinintiro shironi
abisatsatira tsioromento ibashinonketanakerira.
Oshitobakomampeabeta noticieros kapichaji
kamantantsi irokea te añero saikantsi kametsa
Aibetakara añakero ninatantsi;
apinto iñashintsitakabetaro ñanatakobentantsi;
Tsarobantsini inabeta;
Anintakabetaro inkemisanteteme,
antsarobashireabetempa
aikero añaperotanakeari;
Irotaketya, notimabentabetakari noyotakantero,
te iyotakoyetenaro nonkoabetakari nantakante
nonkoasanoti ankemisantabakaya aisankantyari
kametsa

Bislama

translated by Bob Hazen, with assistance from Marie-Therese Serveux

Bob Hazen lives in Oregon where he is a consultant for nonprofit organizations. Earlier in life, he worked in Vanuatu helping with rural development projects, and learned to speak Bislama.

Marie-Therese Serveux lives in Vanuatu, where with eight years of experience, she has served as translator for several major online platforms. She says she loves to do translation work as a way to meet lovely people around the world.

Bislama read by Marie-Therese Serveux

Wan Ofisol Toktok blong Pis

Be from wol ya i wan haos we i stap long faea;
Be from ol nesen oli fulap wetem bigfala singsingaot;
Be from hop i smol, samtaem
wan smol pidjin, hem i stap long waea,
we ol fren blong hem oli fogetem.

Be from ol nius i nomo tokbaot ol kaen fasin
mo pis i wan aedia nomo
be wo i ril;

Be from mi gat ol toktok nomo;
Be from laef blong mi i sot nomo;
Be from mi mi fraet;
Be from mi mi fri—nomata long evri
faea mo kros mo fraet;

Blong stretem nomo wan singsing bae
i kam koling blong mi—wan singsing we oli
no mekem yet hem i wok mo ol toktok blong pis,
bae hem i wok blong mi long ol dei blong
mi we i stap yet.

Bosnian

translated by Adna Mehić

Adna Mehić was born in Tuzla, Bosnia and Herzegovina, and grew up in the Alipašino Polje neighborhood of Sarajevo. She practices several artforms, including a variety of drawing and painting techniques, photography, and dance. Her love of the arts came from her amazing mother, Denisa Mehić. Adna has been a dental technician for five years and loves everything about her job. Though her free time is scarce, she tries to spend it doing things she enjoys.

Evo prevoda:

Dok je svijet kuća u plamenu;
Dok su nacije ispunjene vikom;
Dok se nada čini malom, ponekad
jedna ptica na žici
ostavljena iza migracije.
Dok ljubaznost rijetko dolazi u vijesti
a mir je apstrakcija
dok je rat stvaran;
Dok su riječi sve što imam;
Dok je moj život kratak;
Dok se bojim;
Dok sam slobodan—uprkos svemu
vatri i ljutnji i strahu;
Stoga neka bude odlučeno da će pjesma
biti moj poziv—pjesma
koja još nije stvorena bit će zanimanje
i mirne riječi posao
mojih preostalih dana.

Bulgarian

translated by Gabriela Manova & Rumen Pavlov

Gabriela Manova is a Bulgarian writer, translator, and editor, working between English and Bulgarian. Her poetry collection *Навици/Habits* was published in 2020. Her poems, articles, and translations have been featured in several print and digital editions. In 2023, she was a resident translator at the National Centre for Writing in Norwich, UK.

Rumen Pavlov is a Bulgarian translator, poet, and musician. His first poetry collection in Bulgarian, *Отвор/An Opening* (2020), received a national award for best debut book in 2021. Rumen translates from and to English and has translated mainly U.S. poets into Bulgarian. Along with translating and writing in Bulgarian, he also writes poetry in English.

Bulgarian read by Gabriela Manova

ВЪЗВАНИЕ ЗА МИР

Като знам, че светът е къща във пламъци;
Като знам народите колко крещят;
Като знам, че надеждата е малка, понякога
 самотно птиче на жицата,
 неотлетяло навреме.

Като знам, че доброто рядко е в новините,
 че мирът е абстракция,
 а войната—реалност.

Като знам, че имам само думи;
Като знам, че животът ми е кратък;
Като знам, че съм уплашен;
Като знам, че съм свободен—въпреки
огъня, гнева и страха.

Нека, значи, се реши—песен
 да бъде повикът ми—песен
 още несъздадена да бъде ролята,
 а кротки думи—службата
 на дните ми до края.

Catalan

translated by AKaiser & Jaume C. Pons Alorda

A translator of Catalan, French, and Spanish, AKaiser is the author of *glint* (2020). She recently published poems, translations, and photos in *Amsterdam Quarterly, Circumference, Harvard Review, Poetry International,* and *Poetry.*

Catalan poet and translator Jaume C. Pons Alorda is the author of *Riu, bèstia* (2021) and *Mil súmmuns* (2022). He produced the first complete translation of Walt Whitman's *Leaves of Grass* into Catalan (2014). He has also translated William Wordsworth, Edgar Allen Poe, and Elizabeth Bishop.

Anna Gual is one of Catalunya's most vital poetic voices. From her first book, *Implosions* (2008), to her eighth, *Les ocultacions* (2022), Gual's exploration of the minute to the exponential continues to move and draw in poets, readers, and critics alike. Her *Innombrable*, translated by AKaiser, is forthcoming.

Catalan read by Anna Gual

Una proclamació de pau

Tenint en compte que el món és una casa en flames;
Tenint en compte que les nacions estan
                    plenes de crits;
Tenint en compte que l'esperança sembla
                    petita, talment
un ocell tot sol en un cable elèctric
abandonat durant una migració.
Tenint en compte que l'amabilitat poc o mai surt
                    a les notícies
i la pau és una abstracció
mentre que la guerra és ben real;
Tenint en compte que les paraules són tot el que tinc;
Tenint en compte que la meva vida és curta;
Tenint en compte que tinc por;
Tenint en compte que sóc lliure —malgrat tot
el foc i tota la ràbia i tota la por;
Per tant que tot es converteixi en una cançó
que acabi essent la meva crida—una cançó
encara no feta acabarà essent la meva vocació
i paraules de pau acabaran essent la tasca
dels dies que em queden.

Classical Tibetan/Choekey

The translator of the poem into Classical Tibetan, who is also the translator of the poem into Dzongkha, wishes to remain anonymous.

ཞི་བདེའི་གསལ་བསྒྲགས།

འཛམ་གླིང་མི་ཆེན་གྱིས་ཚོག་པའི་ཁྱིམ་བཞིན།།
རྒྱལ་ཁམས་ཙོ་ཙོ་ཡི་འུར་སྐད་གང་ཆེ།།
སེམས་ཀྱི་རེ་སྒྲོབས་ནི་ཐག་སྲིད་ལ་ཀགས་པའི།།
གྲོགས་མེད་ལུས་པ་ཡི་བྱིའུ་ཅུང་མཆོངས་སོ།།

དུས་འགྱུར་ཡོ་ལང་གྱི་གསར་བསྒྱུར་ནང་དུ།།
བྲམས་བསྟེའི་གདམ་བཟང་ནི་གོ་རྒྱུ་མི་འདུག།
ཞི་བདེའི་གནས་སྟངས་དེ་ཡིད་སློང་ཚམ་དང་།།
དམག་འཁྲུགས་འཐབ་རྩོད་དེ་དངོས་སུ་མཐོང་ཚོ།།

རང་ལ་ཡོད་པ་དེ་སླ་ཚོག་ཚམ་ཞིག།
མི་ཚོ་ཕྱུང་དུ་ཡང་འཛིགས་པས་ཟད་འགྲོ།།
མི་འཛིགས་ཞེ་སྲང་གི་རྒྱབས་ཆ་ཆེ་ཚོ།།
རང་ལག་ཡོད་པ་ཡི་རང་དབང་ལེན་ཏེ།།

ཚོ་འདིའི་དོན་པོ་དུ་བླ་ཚོག་ཚོམ་ཞིང་།།
བརྩམ་འགྱུར་སྐྱེན་བླ་རྣམས་སེམས་ཚོས་བཞིན་དུ།།
ཚོ་འདིའི་སྒྲག་མ་ཞིག་ཏེ་ཚམ་ལུས་པ།།
ཞི་བདེའི་བླ་ཚོག་དེ་སྒྲེལ་ལ་རེམ་འོས།།

Danish

translated by Sinéad Quirke Køngerskov

Sinéad Quirke Køngerskov, PhD, is an award-winning Danish to English translator. In 2022, her translation of *Coffee, Rabbit, Snowdrop, Lost* by Betina Birkjær & Anna Margrethe Kjærgaard (Enchanted Lion) received a Batchelder Honor Award, was listed as a USBBY Outstanding International Book, and was a Kirkus Prize 2022 finalist. She was a literary translation mentee of Allison deFreese in 2020 via the Oregon Society of Translators and Interpreters.

Danish read by Sinéad Quirke Køngerskov

Fredserklæring

Eftersom verden er et hus i brand;
Eftersom nationerne er fyldt med skrig;
Eftersom håbet nogle gange virker lille
en enkelt fugl på en ståltråd
efterladt af migrationen.
Eftersom venlighed sjældent er i nyhederne
og fred er en abstraktion
mens krig er en realitet;
Eftersom ord er alt, hvad jeg har;
Eftersom mit liv er kort;
Eftersom jeg er bange;
Eftersom jeg er fri—trods alt
ild og vrede og frygt;
Derfor skal det besluttes at en sang
skal være min mission—en sang
endnu ikke lavet, skal være mit kald
og fredelige ord arbejdet
i resten af mine dage.

Dutch

translated by Dafne Dahle

Dafne Dahle is a writer, artist, and wanderer in Holland who forsook the practice of the law for a creative life.

Dutch read by Dafne Dahle

Een Verklaring voor Vrede

Terwijl de wereld een brandend huis is;
Terwijl de landen zijn gevuld met geschreeuw;
Terwijl hoop klein lijkt, soms
één enkele vogel op een draad
achtergelaten tijdens de trek.

Terwijl goedheid zelden het nieuws haalt
en vrede abstract is
maar oorlog echt;

Terwijl het enige wat ik heb woorden zijn;
Terwijl mijn leven kort is;
Terwijl ik bang ben;
Terwijl ik vrij ben—ondanks alle
vuur en woede en angst;

Zij het daarom beslecht dat een lied
mijn roeping zal zijn—een lied
nog niet geschreven mijn bestemming
en vredige woorden het werk
van de dagen die mij resten.

Dzongkha

The translator of the poem into Dzongkha, who is also the translator of the poem into Classical Tibetan, wishes to remain anonymous.

གཞི་བདེ

འཛམ་གླིང་མི་གིས་ཆོག་པའི་ཁྱིམ་བཟམ་ན།།
རྒྱལ་ཁམས་ཁ་ཕགས་རྒྱབ་པའི་ཆུར་སྣ་བསྒྱིར།།
བློ་སྟོབས་རེ་བ་ཞག་ཕུ་ཐག་པའི་གུ།།
གློགས་མེད་རང་རྒྱུད་ཡུམ་པའི་བྱེའུ་ཆུང་འད།།

དུས་ཀྱི་འགྱུར་བ་མང་བའི་གནས་ཚུལ་འདུག།
ཞིན་ཏུང་གཏམ་བཟང་ལོ་རྒྱུས་མི་གོ་བས།།
ཞི་བདེའི་གནས་སྟངས་སེམས་ཀྱི་མགོ་བསམ་ཚམ།།
དམག་འཁྲུགས་འཕབ་འཇིང་དངོས་སུ་ལང་པའི་དུས།།

རང་ལུ་ཡོད་པ་ཏུན་པའི་བློ་ཆིག་མས།།
ཚེ་ཐུང་འདི་ཡང་འཇིགས་པས་རྟོགས་པའི་སྐབས།།
མི་འཇིགས་ཞེ་སྡང་ཆུབས་པའི་དུས་ཚོད་ལུ།།
རང་ལུ་ཡོད་པའི་རང་དབང་ཡིན་ཏེ་གིས།།

སྣན་ཆིག་ཚོམ་ནི་མི་ཚེའི་དམིགས་དོན་སྟེ།།
བསྩམ་དགོལ་སྣན་བླུ་སེམས་ཀྱི་ཚོས་སླེ་བཟུང་།།
ཞི་བདེའི་སླེལ་པའི་སྣན་ཆིག་ཚོམ་དེ་གིས།།
མི་ཡུས་ཚོ་ཡི་སྔག་མ་བསླེལ་ད་གོ།།

29

Esperanto

translated by AKaiser

AKaiser is the Pushcart Prize-nominated author of *glint* (Milk & Cake Press), and an NEA-awarded translator of Catalan, French, and Spanish. (You can read more about AKaiser on the Catalan page.)

Proklamo por paco

Dum la mondo estas domo en fajro;
Dum la nacioj estas plenigitaj de krioj;
Dum espero ŝajnas malgranda, foje
ununura birdo sur drato
postlasitaj de migrado.
Dum bonkoreco malofte faras titolojn
kaj paco abstraktaĵo
dum milito estas reala;
Dum vortoj estas ĉio, kion mi havas;
Dum mia vivo estas mallonga;
Dum mi timas;
Dum mi estas libera, malgraŭ ĉio
fajro kaj kolero kaj timo;
Estu tial solvita kanto
ĉi tio estos mia alvokiĝo, ĉi tiu kanto
ankoraŭ ne farita estos voko
kaj pacaj vortoj la laboro
de miaj ceteraj tagoj.

French

freely translated by Anne-Charlotte Giovangrandi

Swiss-born Anne-Charlotte Giovangrandi is an English-to-French freelance translator specializing in patient-facing medical documents, and in marketing materials. She is based in the heart of Silicon Valley.

French read by Anne-Charlotte Giovangrandi

Déclaration de paix

Étant donné que le monde est un incendie,
Que ses pays sont emplis de cris,
Que l'espoir semble ténu, peut-être
un oiseau sur un fil
oublié par ses pairs…
Étant donné que la compassion fait rarement la une,
Que la paix est une abstraction
mais la guerre une dévastation…
Étant donné que je n'ai que mes mots,
Que ma vie est brève,
Que j'ai peur
mais que je suis libre malgré le feu,
la colère et l'angoisse…
Puissions-nous convenir qu'un chant
sera ma vocation, qu'un chant
encore muet m'appellera,
et que je ne vivrai plus
que pour conter la paix.

Gaeilge (Gaelic)

translated by Sinéad Quirke Køngerskov

Sinéad Quirke Køngerskov, PhD, is an award-winning translator of Danish and Gaeilge into English. (You can read more about Sinéad on the Danish translation page.)

Gaelic read by Sinéad Quirke Køngerskov

Forógra na Síochána

Cé gur teach trí thine é an domhan
Cé go bhfuil na náisiúin lán lé béicíl
Cé gur bheag an dóchas, uaireanta
éan amháin ar shreang
arna thréigthe le himirce
Cé nach mbíonn cineáltas sa nuacht go minic
agus gur rud teibí é an tsíocháin
ach is fíor é cogadh;
Cé nach bhfuil faic agam seachas focail;
Cé go bhfuil mo shaol gearr
Cé go bhfuil eagla orm;
Cé go bhfuil mé saor—in ainneoin gach
tine agus fearg agus eagla;
Mar sin beidh amhrán mar mo ghlaoch
– bheidh mo ghlao ina amhrán nach bhfuil
    scríofa fós
agus focail shíochánta an obair
de mo laethanta fágtha.

German

translated by Malcolm Goldman

Malcolm Goldman is a translator and musician based in Portland, Oregon. Their first published translation, *Globus: Studies on the World-Historical Doctrine of Space* by Franz Rosenzweig, came out in 2023. Malcolm has a delightful cat named Bees who provides inner peace during the ups and downs of the times in which we live.

German read by Malcolm Goldman

Eine Proklamation zum Frieden

Während die Welt ein brennendes Haus ist
Nationen mit Brüllen gefüllt
Während die Hoffnung klein erscheint
   Zur Zeit
Ein einsamer Vogel auf der Leitung
Vom Vogelzug entlassen.
Während Menschenliebe selten
In den Nachrichten erwähnt wird
Und Frieden bloß abstrakt,
Krieg ganz wahr,
Mir fehlt alles bis auf die Worte.
Mein Leben ist kurz
Und ich habe Angst
Und ich bin frei–
Trotz aller Feuer, Ärger, Furcht.
Sei es deshalb beschlossen:
Ein Lied wird zu meinem Ruf,
Meinem Beruf–
Ein Lied noch nicht gesungen.
Und friedvoller Ausdruck
Wird jetzt zum Tagewerk
   meiner übrigen Tage.

Greek

translated by Konstantina Velisari

Konstantina Velisari lives in Athens with her beautiful family and works in private practice as a psychologist with teenagers and adults. She is curious about science and art and loves to travel around the world and discover other cultures.

Greek read by Konstantina Velisari

Προκηρύσσοντας την Ειρήνη

Κι ενώ ο κόσμος είναι ένα σπίτι που καίγεται·
Κι ενώ οι λαοί ανταλλάσσουν πυροβολισμούς·
Κι ενώ η ελπίδα φαντάζει ορισμένες στιγμές μικρή,
ένα πουλί μονάχο σε ένα συρματόπλεγμα
ξέχασε να αποδημήσει.
Κι ενώ η καλοσύνη εμφανίζεται σπανίως
   στα νέα
και η ειρήνη αποτελεί αφηρημένη έννοια
ενώ συγχρόνως, ο πόλεμος είναι πραγματικός·
Κι ενώ οι λέξεις είναι όλα όσα έχω·
Κι ενώ η ζωή είναι μικρή·
Κι ενώ φοβάμαι·
Παραμένω ελεύθερη-παρ' όλα αυτά
φωτιά και οργή και φόβος·
Ας είναι η λύση ένα τραγούδι
καθήκον μου αυτό το τραγούδι
προορισμός θα είναι η σύνθεσή του
και η βασική μου δουλειά λόγια ειρηνικά
για το υπόλοιπο της ζωή μου.

Hebrew

translated by Robert Alter

Robert Alter is Professor of Hebrew and comparative literature at the University of California, Berkeley, where he has taught since 1967. He published his translation of the Hebrew Bible in 2018.

Shlomo Libeskind was born in Poland in 1937 and spent the war years in various locations around Warsaw, before emigrating to Israel in 1947, where he later served in the Israeli army during the Sinai campaign. He earned a doctorate in mathematics, and taught in the U.S. and Israel.

Hebrew read by Shlomo Libeskind

הכרזה לשלום

היות והעולם הוא בית עולה באש;
היות והאומות מלאות צעקה;
והתקוה נראית זעירה, לפעמים
צפור יחידה על חוט חשמל
נטושה על-ידי הגירה.

היות והחסד מעט בחדשות
והשלום רק הפשטה
כשהמציאות היא מלחמה;

היות ומלים הן כל מה שיש לי;
היות וחיי קצרים;
היות ואני מפחד;
היות ואני חפשי—למרות כל
האש והזעם והפחד;
לכן יהה השיר
יעודי—שיר
עוד לא עשוי יהיה משימתי
ודברי שלום עבודת
כל ימי הנשארים.

Hungarian

translated by Erika Kóródi

Erika Kóródi was born in Saint Petersburg, Russia and grew up in Budapest, Hungary. She is a certified English, Russian, Hungarian and Spanish conference interpreter, and holds a master's degree in English language and literature. She resides in Budapest with her husband, two daughters, and their dog. And Erika feels honored to see her translation published in this compilation joining colleagues from all over the world.

Hungarian read by Erika Kóródi

Kiáltvány a békéért

Bár lángoló ház a világ,
Bár a nemzetek jajszótól hangosak,
Bár a remény oly kicsi,
    mint dróton a madár,
    kit otthagytak vonuló társai,

Bár ritka hír a jóság,
    s míg elvont a béke,
    valós a háború,

Bár csak szavaim vannak,
Bár rövid az életem,
Bár félek,
Bár szabad vagyok—hiába
    tűz, harag, és félelem,

Eldöntetett, legyen a dal
    a küldetés, legyen a dal—
    mely néma még—a hivatás,
    a békét hozó szó hátralévő
    életem munkája.

Icelandic

translated by Kári Tulinius

Kári Tulinius is an Icelandic poet and novelist. You can find English translations of his stories and poems online. He and his family migrate seasonally between Iceland and Finland like a flock of birds who failed to understand this whole warmer climes business.

Icelandic read by Kári Tulnius

Friðarályktun

Vegna þess að heimurinn er hús í logum
vegna þess að þjóðirnar æpa innbyrðis
vegna þess að vonin virðist svo smá, stundum
eingöngu stakur farfugl á snúru
viðskila við hópinn sem flaug á brott.
Vegna þess að gæska er sjaldan fréttnæm
og friður óáþreifanlegur
á meðan stríð er raunverulegt.
Vegna þess að orð eru allt það sem ég hef
vegna þess að ævi mín er stutt
vegna þess að ég óttast
vegna þess að ég er frjáls—þrátt fyrir
allan eldinn og reiðina og óttann
þá skal ályktað að sönglag
verði mín köllun—sönglag
sem enn er ósamið verður að hugsjón
og friðsöm orð verði verk
þeirra daga sem ég á enn eftir ólifaða.

Italian

translated by Marella Feltrin-Morris

Marella Feltrin-Morris is a freelance translator and professor of Italian at Ithaca College. Her translations of short stories by Luigi Pirandello, Paola Masino, and Massimo Bontempelli have appeared in *North American Review*, *Two Lines*, *Exchanges*, and *Green Mountains Review*.

Italian read by Marella Feltrin-Morris

Dichiarazione di pace

Considerato che il mondo è una casa in fiamme;
Considerato che le nazioni sono sature di grida;
Considerato che la speranza pare poca cosa, a volte
un solo uccello su un filo
dalla migrazione dimenticato.
Considerato che la gentilezza di rado fa notizia
e che la pace è un'astrazione
mentre la guerra è reale;
Considerato che le parole sono tutto ciò che ho;
Considerato che la mia vita è breve;
Considerato che ho paura;
Considerato che sono libero—malgrado tutto
il fuoco e la rabbia e la paura;
Si delibera dunque che un canto
sarà la mia missione—un canto
non ancora composto sarà vocazione
e parole di pace l'opera
dei giorni che mi restano.

Japanese I

translated by Mika Shimizu Jarmusz 清水美香

Mika Shimizu Jarmusz, M.Ed., is an ATA-certified Japanese native translator and a registered court interpreter in the State of Oregon. In her youth, she practiced classical ballet, creative dance, and gymnastics in Japan, where she earned a BA in English as a Foreign Language from KCUFS in Kobe. She then moved to California to study early childhood education, where she observed nonverbal communication at work in a different cultural context.

    Mika is a member of Oregon Society of Translators and Interpreters, and has served as its Director since 2020. She is sometimes recognized as the "button lady" for her collection of antique clothing buttons from around the world. Her portfolio includes leadership training, ISO compliance audits, and marketing to the Japanese audience.

Japanese read by Mika Shimizu Jarmusz

平和宣言

めらめらと火事だ地球が燃えている
あだし国家のいざかいに
はかない夢はぽつねんと
一羽はぐれて電線に
慕うはいずこに群れの空
ニュースが心を見失い
平和は虚ろな言葉の綾
間近に迫るは戦火の渦
そんな身にさえ言葉は宿る
余命はかれこれ見えてきた
どうにも不安でやるせないから
炎火と怒りに負けそうだから
ぼくの言葉がひさかたの
詩（うた）になるならしてみたい。
まだこれからの、そのうたを
ぼくに残ったうつせみの
和（なご）んで平たく世を語る
ぼくの天命にしてみたい。

Japanese II

translated by Liu Jionghao

Liu Jionghao is a doctoral student specializing in translation studies at Binghamton University who is proficient in Chinese, Japanese, and English. Her current research centers on Japanese literary adaptations of Chinese vernacular fiction, especially Shuihuzhuan 水浒传 (Water Margin).

Japanese read by Liu Jionghao

平和への布告

世界は燃えているから；
国々は叫びに満ちているから；
希望は小さく、時にはただ一羽の鳥
渡りの途中に残された電線上の鳥であるから；
善意はほとんどニュースにないから；
戦争だけは現実で
平和は抽象的なものに過ぎないから；
言葉が私の持てる全てであるから；
私の人生は短いから；
私は怖いから；
私は自由であるから―
火と怒りと恐れがあっても；
したがって決意する、歌が私の呼び物となり―
まだ創られていない歌、
平和な言葉が
余生の志事となる。

Kiswahili

translated by Dunia Jospin Mirindi

Dunia Jospin Mirindi is a professional interpreter and translator, and a refugee in Zimbabwe's Tongogara camp. He has worked with the United Nations High Commissioner for Refugees and its implementing partners (such as Red Cross International), the U.S. Citizenship and Immigration Services, the Resettlement Support Center/Africa, and other organizations. He helps the refugee community in Zimbabwe by facilitating communication between them and UN staff.

TANGAZO LA AMANI

Wakati ulimwengu ni nyumba yenye kuwaka moto;
Wakati mataifa zimejaa na kelele nyingi;
Wakati matumaini huonekana kuwa ndogo;
Nyakati nyingine ndege mmoja huachwa nyuma kwenye
    waya wakati wa uhamiaji;
Wakati wema huwa mara chache ndani ya habari na
    amani kutokuwepo;
Wakati vita ni halisi.
Wakati maneno ndio vyote ninavyo;
Wakati maisha yangu ni mafupi;
Wakati nina uoga;
Wakati nipo huru—licha ya moto yote na hasira
    na uoga;
Basi ikitatuliwa wimbo utakuwa wito wangu—wimbo
    ambao hujaundwa bado utakuwa wito wangu
na maneno ya amani kazi ya siku zangu ambazo zimebaki.

Kurdish

translated by Nasrin Mohammed

Nasrin Mohammed is a Core-CCHI and Oregon Health Authority-certified interpreter. She works in Kurdish, Arabic, and English.

Kurdish read by Nasrin Mohammed

راگەیاندنی ئاشتی

لەو کاتەدا جیهان وەکو مالێک لە سوتان دایە
نەتەوەکان پڕن لە هاوار
لە کاتێکدا هیوا زۆر بچوک دیارە هەندێ جار
وەک بالندەیەک لە سەر وایەر
بەجێ مابێ لە ئە نجامی کۆچ کردنەوە
لە کاتێکدا میهرەبانی بە دەگمەن لە هەواڵە کاندا هەیە
وەهەروا لابردنی ئاشتی
لەکاتێکدا جەنگەکە راستەقینەیە
لە کا تێکدا تەنها ووشەکانم هەیە
لە کاتێکدا ماوەی ژینم کورتە
لە کاتێکدا لە مەترسی دام
لە کاتێکدا سەرەرای هەموو شتێک ــ من ئازادم
ئاگرو توورەیی و ترس
وا کار ئەکەن کە لە ئەنجامدا ببن بە گۆرانی
بانگهێشتنامە کەم ببێ بە ــ گۆرانی
هێشتا بانگهێشتنامە کە جێ بە جێ نەکراوە
وە ووشەو کرداری ئاشتی خوازانە
ئە بێتە کارم ماوەی ژیانم

Latin

translated by Simona Gauchers Mancini

Born in Italy, Simona Mancini is a Doctor of Philosophy in Humanities (Ancient History), a translator, and an Old and Modern Literature professor based in Rome. Her first poetry collection *Di madre nuda* (peQuod 2022), semi-finalist in the *Premio Strega Poesia 2023*, has won the *Premio Alma Mater Violani Landi per Opera Prima 2023* from the University of Bologna, and the *Premio Nazionale Letterario Pisa 2023*. The book has been reviewed by both print and online journals. Other lyrics have been published on *Pioggia Obliqua*.

INDICTIO PACIS

Quod domus flagrans est orbis terrarum
Quod clamoribus perfunduntur civitates
Quod tenuis videtur Spes, sola superstes
avis ab advenis aliis deserta.

Quod nobis rarissime humanitatis fama pervenit
Paxque mera cogitatio est cum bellum ipsum sit
Quod mihi supersunt una verba, quod mihi
    brevis est vita,
quod pavesco liberque sum flammis invidia
    metuque neglectis.

Rebus peractis, quid censes?
Ut carmen fiat accitus meus,
nondum scriptum carmen vocatio,
pacifera verba mihi sint
diebus reliquis negotium.
Itaque consentio et conscisco.

Mandarin

translated by Liu Jionghao

Liu Jionghao is a doctoral student specializing in translation studies at Binghamton University, who is proficient in Chinese, Japanese, and English. (You can learn more about Jionghao on the page for Japanese II.)

Mandarin read by Liu Jionghao

一份呼唤和平的宣言

鉴于火势四起；
鉴于各处吵嚷；
鉴于希望力孤势危，
有时就像一只停在电线上的鸟
——被迁徙的鸟群抛下的孤鸟；
鉴于善意少见于新闻，
鉴于战争已在身边而和平止于抽象；
鉴于言辞是我所拥有的一切；
鉴于我的生命短促；
鉴于我害怕；
鉴于我自由
——即使面对着火焰、愤怒和恐惧；
因此宣告，诗歌将是我的呼唤——
未来的诗歌，将承载我的宿命；
和平的话语，将拥有我的余生。

Nepali

translated by Daya Shakya

Born and raised in Naradevi, Kathmandu, Nepal, Daya Shakya is a Nepalese linguist, instructor, interpreter, writer, and social activist for ethnic awareness. Daya has been a leader in Oregon's Newah communities for many years, and has published books including *Newarology Matters* (World Newah Organization, Nepal Chapter, 2024).

Nepali read by Daya Shakya

शान्तिया घोषणा

किम स्टाफोर्ड

सामुहिक बुझाईमा संसार एक अग्नी गृह हो
अनि अर्को तर्फ राष्ट्र एक बुलन्द आवाजले भरेको छ
त्यस्तै आसा त एक सुक्ष्म र सानो लाग्छ
तारमा बसेको एक्लो चरो जस्तो ।
सबैले छोडेर गएको जस्तो देखिने,

जहाँ सम्म दया र मायाको कुरा छ आफै रुप लिने
अनि शान्ति त केवल अलौकिक चित्र ।

तर युद्ध एक सत्य जस्तो लाग्छ

जसबारे केवल मसंग शब्द भण्डार मात्र छ ।

अनि मेरो जिन्दगी केवल अल्प क्षण जस्तो लाग्छ ।

अनि यो आफैमा तर्सिन्छ ।

यस्तै पाराले म स्वतन्त्र भएको ठान्छु - अनेकौं विषयहरु सामु ।

अग्नि राग र भयावह: मात्र

तैपनि एक गीतको आधारशीला छ

व्यक्त गर्न अझै पनि कठिन छ

अनि शान्त वातावरणका शव्दहरु मात्र रुमलिएर अधिकांश मेरा दिनहरु माझ

61

Newar

translated by Daya Shakya & Arun Shrestha

Daya Shakya is a Nepalese linguist. (You can learn more about Daya on the page for Nepali.)

Arun Shrestha is a lecturer at the Campus of International Languages, Tribhuvan University in Kathmandu, Nepal.

Newar read by Arun Shrestha

शान्तिया निंतिं नायेसिं च्ययेके

हिलं जायेक मि च्याना च्वन
दक्को देय् न्यंक चिल्लाये दंगु स: थ्वया च्वन
छुं आस् याये थाय् हे मदु थें च्वं
अले पासापिनिगु बथांनं त्व:ता थकूम्ह
झंग: छम्ह जक छपु तारय् जुया च्वन
माया मतिना धैगु ला आपुलखं सिबे न्यने मन्त
अले शान्ति ला खंके मखनीगु थी हे मफइगु न्यना खँ जक जुल
युद्ध लिछ्याय् मफइगु जुल
जिके धा:सा खँग्व: सिबे छुं मदु
जिगु जीवन चीहाक:
जि ग्या:
अयेजूसां थुज्या:गु मिं, तं व ग्यानापुगु छुकिंनं जित: मपा:
जि स्वतन्त्र
उकिं थौं गनं मदय् धुंकूगु छपु शान्तिया मे हे जिगु बाकि जीवनया आज्जु जुल

63

Norwegian

translated by Bjarne Bjørnevik

Bjarne Bjørnevik is a poet in Norway. His poems address the futility of war, our need for peace, and the quest for dignity and right living in a difficult world.

Norwegian read by Bjarne Bjørnevik

Eit fredsopprop

Ettersom verda er eit hus i brann;
Ettersom nasjonane er fulle
av larm og gny;
Ettersom håpet synest flyktig, stundom
ein fugl åleine på ei snor
skild frå resten av flokken.
Ettersom godheit sjeldan har nyheitsverdi
og fred er ein abstraksjon
medan krig er røynd;
Ettersom ord er alt eg har;
Ettersom livet mitt er kort;
Ettersom eg er redd;
Ettersom eg er fri—trass all
lauseld og vreide og redsle;
Lat det bli kunngjort at ein song
skal vera mitt kall—ein song
som er uferdig mi gjerning
og fredelege ord mitt levebrød
i dagane eg har att.

Pashto

translated by Zaher Wahab

Zaher Wahab attended a village school in his native Afghanistan, before receiving a BA at the American University in Beirut, an MA at Columbia University, and a PhD at Stanford. He then taught anthropology, education, and political economy at Lewis & Clark College in Oregon, from where he took students for overseas study to Sweden, Japan, Portugal, South Korea, Costa Rica, Nicaragua, India, and China, and worked as a Fulbright Scholar in Egypt, Turkmenistan, and Kazakhstan. During the American war in Afghani-stan, he served as a senior advisor to the Minister of Higher Education there, and helped to develop teacher training for Afghan men and women.

Pashto read by Zaher Wahab

سولی په مناسبت یوه څُرگند ونه

څنگه چه نړۍ د یوه کور په شان په اور کی سوځی.
څنگه چه ملکونه له نارو ډک دی.
څنگه چه هیله مندی کمه لیدله کیږی او کله
لکه یواځی مرغه چه له نورو نه
شا ته پاته او په یوه تار ناست وی.
څنگه چه د مهربانۍ نوم ډیر کم اخیست کیږی
او سوله یو خیال او تصور،
لیکن جنگ یو واقعت ده.
څنگه چه ما ته یواځی ویل پاته دی،
څنگه چه زما ژوند لند ده،
څنگه چه زه ویریږم،
څنگه چه زه د ټول اور، غصی، او ویری سره، سره
آزاد یم.
نو څگه دا فیصله او ټینگآر کوم چه له دی وروسته به زما
وجیبه، یوه سندره وی
داسی سندره چه تر اوسه نه ده بلل شوی،
او دا د سولی الفاظ به زما د پاتی ورځو او ژوند
اخلاقی وظیفه، او ده ژوند کرنلاره وی.

Persian

translated by Alireza Taghdarreh

Teacher and translator Alireza Taghdarreh lives in Tehran. He has translated Thoreau's *Walden* into Persion, as well as works by Emerson, William Powers, Kim Stafford, and other U.S. writers. His reflections on Thoreau, Walden, and Persian mystics can be found on YouTube. And special thanks to Persian calligrapher Masoud Eslamifard for gracing this book with artistry.

Persian read by Alireza Taghdarreh

« بیانیه‌ای برای صلح »

از آن روی که جهان خانه‌ای است فرشته ؛

از آن روی که ملت‌ها انباشته از فریادند ؛

از آن روی که امید ناچیزی نمایدو گاه پرنده‌ای است نشسته

بر سیمی و اپس مانده از پرندگان مهاجر .

از آن روی که محبت در خبرها نادر است و صلح ،

خیالی است انتزاعی ؛ حال آن که جنگ واقعی ست ؛

از آن روی که واژه‌ها تمامی دارا یی ‌ام هستند

از آن روی که عمر من کوتاه است ؛ و از آن روی که می‌هراسم

از آن روی که آزاردم ، با وجود تمام آتش و خشم و هراس ،

بگذار تا عهدی ببندم و آرزو کنم ؛

رسالتم سرودی باشد که هنوزکسش نسروده‌ام ؛

و در واپسین روزهای زندگانی‌ام ،

کارم اینکه سخنی از صلح بگویم

خط : مسعود اسلامی نژاد

Polish

translated by Monika Pilecka

Monika Pilecka is an ATA certified freelance translator based in Poland. She graduated from the University of Wrocław (English, Translation Studies) and Kardynal Wyszynski University in Warsaw (Contemporary Polish Editing). A lover of books, cinema, and cats, she lives in Wrocław with her family.

Ravi Raymond Suryan-Beilin, aka Mundo, is of Polish and Indian descent and currently a high school sophomore in Madison, Wisconsin. He plays violin in the Wisconsin Youth Symphony Orchestra and intends to become a marine biologist.

Polish read by Ravi Raymond Suryan-Beilin, aka Mundo

Proklamacja pokoju

Zważywszy, że świat stoi w ogniu jak dom;
zważywszy, że narody rozrywa krzyk;
zważywszy, że nadzieja wygląda niepozornie, czasem
jak samotny ptak na linii energetycznej,
zgubiony przez migrujące stado.
Zważywszy, że o serdeczności rzadko mówią w
wiadomościach,
pokój jest abstrakcją,
a wojna—rzeczywistością;
zważywszy, że słowa są wszystkim, co mam;
zważywszy, że moje życie jest krótkie;
zważywszy, że się boję;
zważywszy, że jestem wolna—mimo
ognia, gniewu i lęku;
czyni się wszystkim wiadome, że pieśń
będzie moim powołaniem—pieśń
niespisana będzie posłannictwem,
a przepełnione pokojem słowa zadaniem
na resztę moich dni.

Portuguese

translated by Scott McClain & Elizabeth Setti Esmay

James (Scott) McClain, lives in Portland, Oregon, with his wife Stella. Scott earned graduate degrees in Public Affairs and Latin American Studies in 1991. He continues to write and study in Spanish and Portuguese. He currently teaches in Portland Public Schools.

Born and raised in Brazil, Elizabeth Setti Esmay moved to the U.S. when she was 23. Her background is in early childhood education, and she has worked as a Spanish and Portuguese interpreter for the public schools since 2014.

Portuguese read by Elizabeth Setti Esmay

Proclamação pela Paz

Enquanto o mundo seja uma casa em chamas;
Enquanto as nações estejam cheias de gritos;
Enquanto a esperança fique pequena, às vezes
   como um pássaro num cabo telefónico
   deixado atrás pela migração.
Enquanto a gentileza raramente aparezca nas
   noticias e a paz seja uma abstração.
Embora que a guerra seja real;
Enquanto palavras são tudo que eu tenho;
Enquanto minha vida é curta;
Enquanto tenho medo;
Enquanto estou livre—apesar de tudo
   esse fogo e raiva e pavor;
Seja resolvido uma canção
   deverá ser minha chamada— uma
   canção ainda não criada deverá ser
   minha vocação e as palavras cheias de
   paz o trabalho dos meus dias restantes.

Punjabi

translated by Moazzam Sheikh & Amna Ali

Born in Lahore, Pakistan, Moazzam Sheikh is a librarian at San Francisco Public Library. He also writes and translates fiction in Urdu, Punjabi, Hindi, and English. He is the author of two collections of short stories: *Cafe Le Whore and Other Stories* and *The Idol Lover and Other Stories of Pakistan*. He was a founding editor of Weavers Press, the U.S.'s only publisher dedicated exclusively to South Asian-American literature in translation.

Amna Ali is the daughter of the noted Punjabi author Nadir Ali. With her husband, Moazzam Sheikh, she collaborated on the anthology *A Letter from India: Contemporary Short Stories from Pakistan* (Penguin, India). She has also co-translated Nadir Ali's works from Punjabi into English for an edition published by Weavers Press titled *Hero and Other Stories* (2022). She is a librarian and lives in San Francisco with her husband and two sons.

Punjabi read by Moazzam Sheikh

کم سٹیفرڈ

جد کہ دنیا اک اگ وچ سڑدا گھراے
تے قوماں چانگھراں ماردیاں ہون
جد کہ آس ماڑی جاپے، کسے ویلے
اک کلا پکھو تار اتے
جنہوں چھڈ گئے ہجرت ویلے.
جد کہ مہردی گل خبراں اندر ویلے کویلے
تے امن خیالی گل ہووے
جدوں جنگ ہووے ٹھوس؛
کیونجے شبد ہی ہین میرے کول؛
جد کہ حیاتی میری کم ہے
جد کہ میں ڈردا ہاں؛
جد کہ میں آزاد ہاں ـــــ باوجود
اگ تے کرودھ تے ڈر دے؛
اے تاں ٹھان لئی کہ اک گاون
میری کوک ہوسی۔ اوہ گاون
جہڑا حالی پنگھریا نئیں میرا پیشہ ہوسی
تے امن دے بول میرا کم
میری رہندی حیاتی تائیں.

Quechua (Cusco-Collao)

translated by Guipsy Alata Ramos

Guipsy Alata Ramos is a Quechua interpreter and translator from Peru, and a lawyer by profession. Her work involves activities related to linguistic rights, intercultural justice, the rights of indigenous or native peoples, interculturality, and public administration. She currently works as a specialist in Promoting Intercultural Focus through the Peruvian Ministry of Culture's General Board of Intercultural Citizenship.

Quechua read by Guipsy Alata Ramos

Thak kawsaypaq willakuy

Nina ninapi wasi hina tiqsimuyu kaqtin;
Qapariykuna nacionkunata wasapaqtin;
Suyakuyqa huch'uylla hina rikch'akuqtin,
sapa kuti k'anchachiq cable patapi
saqisqa ch'ulla urpi puñun.
Noticia willakuykunapi pisiña sumaq
sunqu hinallataq thak mana yuyayniyuq kaqtin
Awqanakuy chiqaqña kashan chaypas;
Simillawanmi kaqtiy;
Kawsayniy pisilla kaqtin;
Manchakuqtiy;
Qispiyuq kaqtiy, ninapas, phiñaypas
hinallataq manchakuy kaqtinpas;
Chaynaya, harawi allinchay
ruwaysikuyniymi kanqa, manaraq
ruwasqa harawi ruwayniy kanqa
hinallataq tukuy kawsayniypi thak
rimaykunata llamk'ayniymi kanqa.

Romani

translated by Agnieszka Caban, with assistance from Roksana Jessica Mroczek and Patrycja Jenny Mroczek

Agnieszka Caban is a Polish scholar, editor, curator, and translator dedicated to cultural dialog, and advocacy for ethnic minorities, particularly the Roma.

Maria Luiza Medeleanu teaches Romani culture and literature at the University of Bucharest, where she writes on the ethics of fictionality and cultural identity of the Roma.

Romani read by Maria Luiza Medeleanu

Wyziakirdo łokhiben

Uław de siero, kaj sweto sy kher de jaga;
Uław dre siero, kaj miśtypen sy ceło dre godli;
Uław dre siero, kaj na ni ćsi pe so te ziakireł,
    so sawoś cyro
Jek ćryklo ćhija ziakireł
A łeskro kher dur kaj wawir te.

Uław dre siero, kaj łatćhiben phares te siuneł
A łokhipen hara nani
De cyro de sawo maryben dzido dadyves;

Uław dre siero, kaj ława sy saro so, man sy;
Uław dre siero, kaj dzijipen miro na jaweła hara;
Uław dre siero, kaj man daraw
Uław dre siero, kaj som pe frejda—paś da sare
jaga, holina i dar;

Daw ław, kaj gili
jaweła miro kharyben—gili
dadyves na kerdy jaweła miry buty
i łaćsie ława ćsinawa
ke meryben.

Romanian

translated by Ileana Marin

Ileana Marin teaches interdisciplinary courses at the University of Washington, and at the University of Bucharest. She has published books on tragic myths, Pre-Raphaelite artists, and Victorian aesthetics of erasure. Since 2020, she has taken on translating Romanian female writers who are underrepresented in English.

Romanian read by Ileana Marin

O Proclamație pentru pace

Când lumea e o casă în flăcări,
Când națiunile se umplu de țipete,
Când speranța pare mică,
uneori o pasăre stingheră pe sârmă
rămâne în urma stolului migrator.
Când bunătatea e rareori la știri
și pacea, o abstracțiune,
în vreme ce războiul e real,
Când cuvintele sunt tot ce am,
Când viața mea e scurtă,
Când mă tem,
Când sunt liberă—
În ciuda focului, mâniei și fricii;
Să fie cântecul chemarea mea—
un cântec neînceput,
să fie vocația,
iar cuvintele de pace,
lucrarea zilelor mele rămase.

Russian

translated by Gleb & Vita Sapozhnikov

Gleb and Vita are healthcare interpreters. As native Russian speakers, they share memories of the USSR, where they were born and raised. Gleb, originally from Kyiv, studied in St. Petersburg before pursuing a BS in computer engineering at Kyiv Polytechnic Institute. Vita, born in Moscow, spent her childhood in both Kyiv and Maykop before attending Sofia State University in Bulgaria, where she became a Bulgarian speaker and earned a BA in linguistics.

    Their paths crossed in Kyiv against the backdrop of the Soviet Union collapsing, with Gleb having already moved to the U.S., and traveling to meet Vita in Sofia, where they married. Gleb renewed his Ukrainian roots, while Vita expanded her linguistic repertoire to include English, Ukrainian, Polish, Japanese, French, and Greek. Their U.S. story has unfolded with three children, and relocating to Oregon.

Russian read by Gleb Sapozhnikov

МАНИФЕСТ О МИРЕ

Ибо мир—это дом в огне,
Ибо народы полнятся криками,
Ибо надежда едва жива и порой
　　подобна одинокой птице на проводах,
　　от которой улетела стая,

Ибо доброта редко появляется в новостях,
　　а мир—это абстракция,
　　тогда как война — реальна;

Ибо слова — это всё, что у меня есть,
Ибо жизнь моя коротка,
Ибо мне страшно,
Ибо я свободен — назло всему
　　огню, гневу и страху, —

Посему да будет решено, что песнь
　　станет моим призванием — песнь
　　ещё не созданная станет зовом,
　　а мирные слова—трудом
　　оставшихся мне дней.

Spanish (Latin American)

translated by Romina Espinosa

Romina Espinosa was born on the Peruvian coast during a Southern Hemisphere summer. She is a creative writer, Spanish-English interpreter, and translator living in San Diego, California. Romina holds degrees from the University of California at San Diego and the University of Oviedo in Spain. She is a curious lefty who loves nature runs, abstract art, farmers markets, and seeing the world.

Spanish (Latin American) read by Romina Espinosa

Proclamación de Paz

Cuando una casa en llamas es el mundo;
Cuando los gritos colman las naciones;
Cuando la esperanza parece minúscula,
con frecuencia yace una paloma
abandonada por la bandada
sobre un cable de luz.
Cuando escasa es la amabilidad en noticieros
y la paz elemento abstracto
Si bien la guerra es una realidad;
Cuando tengo solo palabras;
Cuando corta es la vida mía;
Cuando temo;
Cuando tengo libertad, a pesar de
las llamas e ira y el temor;
Así pues, resolver un canto
deber mío será, un canto
aún no compuesto será mi oficio
y la labor por el resto de mi vida
labrar palabras pacíficas.

Spanish (world)

translated by D. P. Snyder

D. P. Snyder is a bilingual writer and Spanish translator. Her work has appeared in *The Southern Review, Ploughshares, Two Lines Journal* and *World Literature Today*. Her book-length works include *Meaty Pleasures* by Mónica Lavín (Katakana Editores, 2021), *Arrhythmias* by Angelina Muñiz-Huberman (Literal Publishing & Hablemos, escritoras, 2022), and *Scary Story by* Alberto Chimal (Pamenar Press, 2023).

Spanish read by D. P. Snyder

Declaración de paz

Considerando que el mundo es una casa en llamas;
Considerando que las naciones se llenan de griteríos;
Considerando que la esperanza parece diminuta,
a veces un ave solitaria en un cable
abandonado por su bandada migrante.
Considerando que el noticiero rara vez trata
    de la bondad
y la paz es una abstracción
mientras la guerra es manifiesta;
Considerando que las palabras son lo único
    que tengo;
Considerando que mi vida es corta;
Considerando que tengo miedo;
Considerando que estoy libre a pesar de todo
fuego, rabia y temor;
Por lo tanto, que se resuelva que un canto
será mi vocación, un canto
aún no compuesto será vocación
y vocablos de paz serán la labor
de los días que me quedan.

Swedish

translated by Henrik Otterberg

Henrik Otterberg has co-translated Swedish poems by Ingela Standberg and Tomas Tranströmer into English. He wrote his PhD on Thoreau's aesthetics and served as bibliographer of the Thoreau Society (Concord, Massachusetts) and its quarterly publication *Thoreau Society Bulletin*.

En Appell för Fred

Emedan världen är ett hus i lågor;
Emedan nationerna fylls av gap och glåp;
Emedan hoppet känns litet, så lämnas ibland
en ensam fågel kvar på eltråden
av flyttlasset.

Emedan godhet sällan får plats bland nyheterna;
och förblir en abstraktion
medan kriget är verkligt;

Emedan ord är allt jag har;
Emedan mitt liv är kort;
Emedan jag är rädd;
Emedan jag är fri—trots all

eld och ursinne och rädsla;
Varde det därför bestämt att en sång
skall bli mitt kall—en sång
ännu ej skriven skall bli mitt arbete
och fredliga ord min syssla
dessa återstående dagar.

Tagalog

translated by Su Layug

Su Layug has been a professional Tagalog translator and interpreter for two decades. She is also a creative writer who has won awards for her personal essays, both in the Philippines and in the U.S., including the Carlos Palanca Memorial Awards for Literature and the Ray Bradbury Creative Contest. Her poetry and personal essays have been published online and in print, with one of them used for teaching K-12 creative writing in the Philippines. Her nonfiction and poems have been picked up by independent publishers on *Medium*, an online literary blog. She has been blogging about English-Filipino literary translation on WordPress for years and hopes to someday publish a full-length book of translations.

Tagalog read by Su Layug

Isang Proklamasyon para sa Kapayapaan

Bagaman at dahil isang nagliliyab na bahay
   ang mundo;
Dahil at bagaman sukdulan ang mga bansa
   sa sigawan;
Bagaman at dahil wari'y maliit ang pag-asa, minsa'y
nag-iisang ibon lamang sa kawad
na napag-iwanan ng migrasyon.
Dahil at bagaman bihira ang kagandahang-loob
   sa balita
at isang ideyang halaw lamang ang kapayapaan
habang ang digmaan nama'y tunay;
Bagaman at dahil mga salita lamang ang taglay ko;
Dahil at bagaman maikli lamang ang buhay ko;
Bagaman at dahil natatakot ako;
Dahil, bagaman, sapagkat ako'y malaya—
   sa gitna ng lahat
ng apoy at galit at takot;
Kung kaya sa gayo'y napagpasyahan na isang awit
ang aking magiging lunggati—isang awit
na hindi pa buo ang siyang magiging bokasyon
at mapapayapang salita ang magiging likhain
ng mga nalalabi ko pang araw.

Tamil

translated by Prabu Muruganantham

Prabu Muruganantham grew up in a small farming village in the South Indian state of Tamil Nadu. He immigrated to Portland, Oregon, in 2014. Literature, philosophy, and filmmaking are his interests. Prabu serves on the board of Portland-based prison arts nonprofit Open Hearts Open Minds. During the pandemic, he interviewed and consulted with several former inmates on their experience returning to society, and made his first short narrative film. This is his first translation project.

Tamil read by Prabu Muruganantham

அமைதியின் முரசு

உலகு எனும் இல் எரிய,
தேசங்கள் கூக்
குரல்களில் நிறைய,
உறுதி சிறுத்து, வலசை
விட்டுச் சென்ற
ஒற்றைத் தனிப்
பறவையாய் நிற்க.
இரக்கம் அரி பொருளாக,
அமைதி கருத்தொன்றேயாக,
போர் மட்டும் நிதர்சனமாக
எஞ்சிய இச் சிறு வாழ்வில்
அஞ்சிய என்னுள்
எஞ்சியது
வெறுஞ் சொற்கள்.
இவ் வெறி, சினம், அச்சம்
கடந்து நான்
சுதந்திரமானவன். எனவே,
இதுவரை இயற்ற படாத
பாடல் ஒன்றை என்
வினை எனக்
கொள்கிறேன்,
அமைதியின் சொற்களை
எஞ்சிய என் நாட்களின்
பணி என.

Thai

translated by Piyawee Ruenjinda & Jeta Jiranuntarat

Piyawee and Jeta, mother and son co-translators, were raised in a family that deeply appreciates the value of language, with family members daily composing and sharing poems. Both Piyawee and Jeta engage with language in a playful manner, finding joy in its nuances. They are both pacifists and passionate about social justice. They feel honored to be part of this project and to faithfully translate the poem into Thai.

Thai read by Piyawee Ruenjinda

คำประกาศเพื่อสันติภาพ

ขณะที่โลกเสมือนบ้านในกองเพลิง
ขณะที่นานาชาติอื้ออึงด้วยเสียงตะเบ็งร้อง
ขณะที่ความหวังดูริบหรี่ บางครั้ง
นกตัวเดียวเกาะสายไฟ
ถูกฝูงอพยพทอดทิ้งให้เดียวดาย
ขณะที่ความกรุณาขาดหายในข่าว
สันติภาพเป็นเพียงนามธรรม
ในขณะที่สงครามเป็นเรื่องจริง
เนื่องจากคำพูดเป็นสิ่งเดียวที่ฉันเหลืออยู่
เนื่องจากชีวิตของฉันสั้นนัก
เนื่องจากฉันหวาดหวั่น
เนื่องจากฉันเป็นอิสระ—แม้รายล้อม
ด้วยเปลวเพลิง โทสะ และความหวาดหวั่น
จึงต้องหันมาแก้ไขภายในด้วยบทเพลง
จักเป็นเสียงเพรียกของฉัน—บทเพลง
ที่ไม่เคยเอื้อนเอ่ย จักเป็นการงาน
และคำพูดเพื่อสันติจะเป็นพันธกิจ
ในวันเวลาที่ฉันเหลืออยู่

Turkish

translated by F. Gülşen Buecher

F. Gülşen Buecher is a Turkish-American poet living in Santa Cruz, California. She grew up in Brooklyn, New York, and earned degrees in English and Law before pursuing creative writing and translation full-time.

Turkish read by F. Gülşen Buecher

Barış İlanı

Halbuki dünya yanan bir ev gibidir;
Halbuki ulusar bağırmak doluyken;
Halbuki sanki ümit kuçuk, bazen telin
üzerindeki kuş gibidir,
geride bırakılmış.
Halbuki iyilik haberlerde pek çıkmaz
ve barış bir soyutlama
sırasında harp hakikidir;
Halbuki tek sözlerim var;
Halbuki benim hayatım kısa;
Halbuki korkuyorum;
Halbuki özgürlüğüm var— tum öfkeye,
korkuya, ve yagına rağmen;
Bu yüzden çözülmüş olsun
bir şarkı benim görevimdir— daha yazılmamış
bir şarkı benim mesleğimdir
ve kalan günlerim barış kelemeler olmalıdır.

Ukrainian

translated by Iana Ianovska

Iana Ianovska is a linguist (Ukrainian, English, German, Russian) and a psychologist. Iana currently resides in Germany where she works as a psychologist and a research assistant at the Clinic for Psychiatry, Psychotherapy, and Psychosomatics, at Augsburg District Hospital.

Ukrainian read by Iana Ianovska

Послання миру

Коли світ охоплений полум'ям;
Коли нації сходять на крик;
Коли майже немає надії -
вона як одинока птаха на дроті, залишена своєю зграєю.
Коли доброта рідко з'являється в новинах,
Коли мир—абстрактна ідея,
А війна—реальна.
А в мене немає нічого, крім слів;
І моє життя коротке;
І мені страшно;
І все ж я вільний всупереч вогню, і гніву, і страху;
То ж вирішено: моїм покликанням буде пісня—ще не написана пісня стане моєю долею,
а слова миру—працею залишених мені днів.

Upper Austrian (a dialect of the Central Bavarian language family)

translated by Carola F. Berger

Carola F. Berger is an ATA-certified German into English and English into German patent and science translator with a PhD in physics and an MA in engineering physics. She grew up in a small town in Upper Austria, but has been living in the U.S. for most of her adult life. The translation of this poem is an attempt to rediscover her roots.

Upper Austrian read by Carola F. Berger

A Friednsproklamation

Leitln—Auf da Wöt, do brennt da Huat.
Leitln—De Schrei, de gengan bis ins Bluat!
Leitln—De Hoffnung, de is winzig klaa,
wia a Vogerl am Drohtseul,
vagessn vom Schwoam und gonz alaa.

Leitln—In de Schlogzeun zagn's des Guate nie,
nua Kriag und imma de Pandemie.
De Bombn, de san echt—ka Friedn,
    imma nua Gefecht.

Leitln—I kå eich nua des Woat mitgebn;
Leitln—weu vü zu kuaz is es, des Lebn.
Leitln—Monchmoi wiad ma ångst und bång;
Leitln—frei bin i—trotz ollem Zwång!

Deshoib sei beschlossn, dass a afochs Liad,
soi ma genga gånz bis ins Gmiat.
Und da Rest vo meinem Lebn
sei dem Liadl hingegebn!

Vietnamese

translated by Ms. Tram Bui & Mr. Hai Tran

Tram Bui is a National Board Certified Medical Interpreter and a translator working in Vietnamese and English. She is the lead moderator for the SE Asian Languages Special Interest Group of the American Translators Association. She is also a trainer for the nonprofit Americans Against Language Barriers. She resides in the Phoenix, Arizona, area with her son. She loves all things language-related and enjoys traveling and trying out new restaurants.

Hai Tran is a native Vietnamese translator living in Hanoi. He has worked in the translation industry for 20 years and has translated many books from English into Vietnamese, including Jared Diamond's *Collapse: How Societies Choose to Fail or Succeed* and Bill McGuire's *Global Catastrophes: A Very Short Introduction.*

Vietnamese read by Tram Bui

Lời Khẩn Cầu Cho Hoà Bình

Khi cả thế giới như ngôi nhà đang cháy;
Khi các quốc gia ngập tràn những tiếng la hét;
Khi niềm hy vọng chỉ còn là thứ nhỏ nhoi, như
một chú chim lẻ loi trên dây điện
bị rớt lại trong một cuộc di cư.
Khi lòng tốt chẳng còn trên các bản tin
và hòa bình trở nên mờ ảo
khi chiến tranh đang bùng nổ khắp nơi;
Khi lời nói là tất cả những gì tôi có;
Dù cuộc đời tôi ngắn ngủi;
Dù tôi lo sợ;
Nhưng tôi tự do – vượt qua tất cả
Những ngọn lửa, căm giận và sợ hãi;
Hãy cất cao tiếng hát
là lời kêu gọi của tôi - một bài hát
vẫn chưa được viết thành sẽ là một ơn gọi
và những từ ngữ dịu êm sẽ là công việc
trong những ngày còn lại của đời tôi.

Yoruba

translated by Abayomi Animashaun

Abayomi Animashaun is the author of three poetry collections and editor of three anthologies. He is an Assistant Professor of English at the University of Wisconsin Oshkosh, and a poetry editor at *The Comstock Review*.

Yoruba read by Abayomi Animashaun

Ikede fun Alafia

Nitori pe gbogbo aye n jona
Nitori pe gbogbo orile ede n pariwo
Nitori pe ireti dabipe otitan, nigba miran
eye kan shosho
le ba le oke ile.
Nitori pe ife showon ninu iroyin
be naa ni alafia showon
ogun si po pelu;
Nitori pe ewi nikan ni mo ni
Nitori pe ojo ori mi ko po mo
Nitori pe eru si n bami;
Nitori pe mo shi ni ominira—nigba
ijona ati ibinu ati ijaya;
Nitori naa, orin yii
Ni o je ipe mi—orin
Itura ti a n wa pelu oro alafia
Ni mo ma maa ko l'ojojumo
Titi ojo aye mi.

Yucatec Maya

translated by Lizbeth Carrillo Can

Originally from Peto (Yucatan, Mexico), Lizbeth Carrillo Can is a native Yucatec Maya speaker, translator, and instructor. Since 2002, Liz has promoted Mayan language acquisition and literacy by teaching courses for the Board of Indigenous Education, at the Itzamná Municipal Academy of Mayan Languages, the Yucatec Maya Institute, at the UADY's (Autonomous University of the Yucatán) Language Institute Center, and at other institutions. She has developed literary materials for Mayan-speaking communities through El Instituto Nacional de Educación para Adultos (2004), and edited the book *Elementos Esenciales del idioma Maya* (Ayuntamiento de Mérida, 2015).

Yucatec Maya read by Lizbeth Carrillo Can

K'a'aytajt'aan yo'olal ets'a'an óolal

Tukulta'ake' yóok'olkaabe' jump'éel naj táan u yelel;
Tukulta'ake' tu kaajilo'ob yóok'olkaabe' tataj
    aawat ku yúuchuli';
Tukulta'ake' yaan k'iine' alab óolale' ku bin
    u jump'íittal,
juntúul ch'íich tu juunal t'uchukbal tu suumil *cable*
xúump'atta'ab tumen u yéet máani'máan
    ch'íich'ilo'ob.
Tukulta'ake' utsil ba'alo'obe' óol ma' mantats'
    ku k'i'itbesa'al noticiasi',
ets'a'an óolale' istikyaaj u na'ata'al jach ba'axi'
ba'ax jach táan u yúuchule' ba'ate'eltáambalil;
Tukulta'ake' chéen ja'alil t'aano'ob ku jaajtal
    tin kuxtal;
Tukulta'ake' in kuxtale' mix chowaki';
Tukulta'ake' saajaken;
Tukulta'ake' ku páajtal in beetik ya'ab ba'al tumen
    ma' paliltsilta'aneni'
kex yéetel tóoch'balil, muk'ulmuuk' yéetel
    kikil óolalil;
Le o'olal ichil jump'éel k'aay kun jóok'ol
leti' ba'ax in k'áat, jump'éel k'aay
kex mix patjo'olta'ake', leti' ba'ax in k'áat
yéetel u t'aanilo'ob éets'a'an óolal.
tak tu xuul u k'iinilo'ob in kuxtal.

Zapotec

translated by Fr. Eleazar López Hernández

Fr. Eleazar López Hernández is a Roman Catholic priest and a member of the Zapotec Indian community of the Isthmus of Tehuantepec, Oaxaca, Mexico. He has worked in indigenous ministry since 1970; he is a cofounder of the Movement of Indigenous Priests of Mexico and a member of the Ecumenical Association of Third World Theologians. In the 1990s he served as an advisor to the commission that mediated between the Mexican government and the Zapatista rebels. And in 2019, Pope Francis called on him as an expert in Indigenous Theology for the Pan Amazonian Synod. His articles have appeared in theological magazines in Mexico, Costa Rica, Bolivia, Ecuador, Argentina, France, Italy and Germany.

Zapotec read by Fr. Eleazar López Hernández

Uguánu hridxi: chu´ Guendanazaaca

Pa caya´qui´ ti yoo, guirá´ yoo caya´qui´
Pa nuu yuuba´ ladxido´binni guidxilayú
Pa ma zirá guendaribéza xiixa,
Gúguhuiini´ ma nexhedxí layú
bisaanarenda xcaadxi gúguque laa
yetíca´ lú ti guiiba´ zené biaani´.
Pa cará guendanayéche´ hra ruzeetecabe
        ni cazaaca
ne guendanazaaca ma ziné bí laa
ne nisi guendaridínde nácabe nuu guidxilayú.
Xísi nga naa náparua´diidxa´ guinié´
neca ma zirá guendabani xtinne´.
Dxi naa cadxíbe´
dxi guirúti´naaze naa
ne názebele guendaridxiichi ne guendaridxibi
Naa rábe´: zuundarua´
ti ngá nga dxiiña´zanda gúne´
ne cá ique´ zúne´ biá tiica dxí guibáne´
zucheeche´ diidxa´ gúni guibiguéta´
        Guendanazaaca

Afterword
by Kim Stafford

I wrote "A Proclamation for Peace" during a faculty meeting at my school. As we discussed the budget and other matters of administration, my colleague Zaher stood and said, *The world is on fire—and we are dithering with these details?* The poem then came to the page out of my longing for peace for all people, and for Earth. Isn't this what our children deserve from us?

Since that day, the poem has been set to music, printed as a letterpress broadside, read as a blessing at a conference for journalists in danger, and appeared in the poetry collection *Wild Honey, Tough Salt*. Now, by this project, "A Proclamation for Peace" has traveled around the world. Thanks to the vision of Allison deFreese at the Oregon Society of Translators and Interpreters, this project has gathered the devotional work of translators far and wide— translators have, in fact, created many new poems seeded by my own, thus planting a garden of songs.

I am deeply grateful to Allison for her vision and persistent follow-through to bring this book to press, and to all our translators who gave their time, care, and expressive voice to this project.

Scholars have long shared the idea that essential elements of a text will disappear in translation. It has even been said that "Poetry is what gets lost in translation," that lyric essence can't cross the gap between one language and another. But I believe the opposite may be true. In the process of this project, I've seen my humble text cause new poems to be written in languages around the world. So I have written this poem for my friends at work with the translator's art:

Found in Translation

Without a deft interpreter in court,
how can we learn the story of innocence?
Without a translator in care, how can we
know the story of pain: *Me duele aquí.*
So might translation make the story born
in my tongue grow stronger in another—
to make of mutter, song, of feathers, flight?
Might translation take my poem, clumsy,
half-made, and help it soar across the chasm?
Might translation turn my blur, my rugged
guess, into insight clear as mountain water
sipped slowly by children everywhere
                to savor syllables of luck?

By the many voices in this book, may poetry be the "wind horse" carrying peace to all sentient beings around the world.

Notes on languages in this book, the work of translation, and reflections by our translators.

A note on Arabic by El Habib Louai
The ultimate motive behind my unconditional engagement with Mr. Stafford's poem is attributable to the fact that it states its intentions unequivocally. In other words, it respectively invites me, as a translator, to enter what Gayatri Spivak calls the ethico-political arena where I decide, as a consciously linguistic intermediator with a universal worldview, to embrace its outcries for peace, justice, brotherly humaneness, and unconditional reverence of the subject/self in a world dismembered by territorial greediness, nationalistic chauvinism, and religious fanaticism. My translation of Mr. Stafford's poem was prompted by its extolment of common values such as justice, equality, and love which is the only value that we need in times of adversity.

A note on Armenian by Vardan Aslanyan
This poem contains a simple yet powerful description of the realities of war. The author is full of hope, and is resolved to proclaim and defend Peace, which is such a universal and truthful goal. Sounding encouraging in Armenian, and they naturally produced rhyme.

A note on Ashaninka by Marilu Iroba Cipriani
For me, the translation of this poem was somewhat

complicated given its message, though translating it was not impossible. The poem reflects the harsh reality many countries are experiencing where, in many cases, justice is nowhere to be found and living in Peace is not possible. At the same time, the poem will give increased visibility to original languages (such as Ashaninka). I applaud the poet for his commendable work.

<u>A note on Bislama by the editors</u>
Bislama is an English lexifier-creole language related to Pijin of the Solomon Islands and Tok Pisin of Papua New Guinea. It is also the official language of Vanuatu—an archipelago of 82 volcanic islands in Oceania. Around 10,000 people (or fewer) speak Bislama as a first language, with around 200,000 second-language speakers. With most of its islands at or near sea level, Vanuatu is one of the world's nations most at risk from climate change.

<u>A note on Bosnian by the editors</u>
Bosnian is one of three related language variations spoken in Bosnia and Herzegovina, along with Serbian and Croatian. It is a recognized minority language in several surrounding countries. Though Bosnian and Serbian share nearly identical vocabulary and grammar structures, the two languages use different alphabets.

Notes on Bulgarian by Gabriela Manova & Rumen Pavlov

Gabriela: What I found especially challenging in the translation of "A Proclamation for Peace" was the rendition of "calling" and "vocation," which in Bulgarian have very similar meanings. My final choices were words, the closest translations of which would be "role"/"purpose" and "service." I feel they capture the initial intent.

Rumen: At first I was wondering which meaning of "whereas" to choose, until "therefore" in the final part made me translate it in the sense of "having in mind"—with everything after "therefore" serving as a resolution. As its literal translation in Bulgarian would be too clumsy, I chose "As I know…."

A note on Catalan by AKaiser

It's always enjoyable, and challenging, to collaborate on a translation. There are myriad ways to hear the original text, and varying ways to convey it. I believe Jaume and I came to an understanding, both of us giving and receiving in the process. For myself, two things drew me right into Kim Stafford's "A Proclamation for Peace." One, the title (what poet would dare such a feat, and of what would it consist?); two, the first word, "whereas," and this, in turn, for two reasons: one being my past employment with the UN, where I both wrote documents starting with this significant word, and read many more; the other being that one of my repeat-read poetry collections is *Whereas* by Layli Long Soldier (Graywolf Press, 2017). You might even say there was some assumption on my part that this poem would indeed have political import. This week, I was also reading *Up Late* by Nick Laird (Norton, 2024), a collection where "fire" is a key word, and here we are again, in this poem, in this "house on fire." So many fires. May these words of peace, and others, help to extinguish them.

A note on Classical Tibetan (Choekey) by the editors
Texts of Tibetan Buddhism are written in Choekey, or Classical Tibetan—the language of Dharma. Choekey was once a lingua franca as well as a clerical and diplomatic language for much of central Eurasia, and remains a core element of Tibet's national identity. It is spoken by 150,000 Tibetan exiles in India and elsewhere.

A note on Danish by Sinéad Quirke Køngerskov
"A Proclamation for Peace" is not so much a poem, as it is a poetic declaration of intent—the words in English are simple, there is an "economy" to them. Yet, those words carry profound determination—kindness and peaceful words are what the world needs in practice, not in abstraction. It is said that what we focus on becomes our reality, so by focusing on peace, a song not yet made, as something concrete, peace can be a reality.

The Danish translation is quite literal. The challenge was the "resolution"—the syntax is distinct in English. The same inversion could not be captured in Danish, particularly as I wanted to keep the same economy of words. The solution was to make the sentence quite straightforward, which suits the poem in Danish. It is, after all, a proclamation.

<u>A note on Dutch by the editors</u>
A West-Germanic language, Dutch is the national language of the Netherlands, and one of the three official languages of Belgium, where it is known as "Flemish" (*Vlaams*). Dutch, which has both standard (Standaardneder-lands or Algemeen Nederlands) and dialectal forms, is also the language of administration in Suriname, Curaçao, Sint Maarten, Aruba, Bonaire, Saba, and Sint Eustatius, which once made up the Netherlands Antilles. Afrikaans, a derivative of Dutch, is an official language of South Africa.

In the Middle Ages the language was called *Dietsc* or *Duutsc*, meaning simply "language of the people," in contrast to Latin, which was the language of religion and learning. The earliest documents in the Dutch language date from approximately the end of the 12th century.

The Dutch language can be very challenging for native English speakers to pronounce correctly as many of the sounds used don't exist in English. *Doei doei!*

A note on Dzongkha by the editors
In 1961, King Jigme Dorji Wangchuck decreed Dzongkha the national language of Bhutan with the aim of creating one linguistic identity for the country. Until that decree, there had been no official language policy in Bhutan. No spoken language was a national language because none of the spoken Tibeto-Burman languages had developed into a written language.

A note on English by the editors
English, a West Germanic language, is the most widely spoken language in the world, primarily due to the influence of the former British Empire (and later the Commonwealth of Nations), and the U.S. English is the third-most spoken native language (with about 380 million speakers) after Mandarin, Chinese, and Spanish. English has more second-language speakers than native speakers (over a billion).

English is either the official language of or an official language of 59 sovereign states. It is also an official language of the UN, the EU and many other international organizations. It is the de facto global lingua franca. For instance, all pilots must be able to communicate in English regardless of their native language.

A note on Esperanto by AKaiser
Esperanto, the language, whose name means "one who

hopes," is called a "constructed" language, and was created in 1887 by the Pole L.L. Zamenhof. I became newly interested in it thanks to an exposition in Barcelona on "Revolutionary Catalunya" (July 1936– May 1937), a time when the area coexisted with an array of actors. To include the variegated members of the power structure, the Catalan self-governing Generalitat would publish governmental documents in several languages, including Esperanto. This past spring, but for a passport snafu, I was to present on these facts in Spain. It is for this paper that I began exploring the language itself. I would say the biggest frustration as a newcomer to "one who hopes" is not the verb tenses—this aspect of Esperanto reminded me of Chinese—but vocabulary issues, including the more grammatical point of the absence of the indefinite article. In the first case, was I to repeat "calling" because for "vocation," only "call" repeatedly came up as an option? It helped, I believe!, when I switched the order of these two words. As for the fourth line from the end of the poem, I added one "this" for clarity, but then ended up liking the rhythm of repeating the "this" at the beginning and at the end of the poem alike, as a way to emphasize the steadfast resolve of the speaker's promise, the strength of this evolving song.

<u>A note on French by Anne-Charlotte Giovangrandi</u>
Even though I strive to translate with style, I am not a

literary translator, and I had never translated poetry. But I love the enriching experience offered by collaborative translation. So when I heard OSTI was organizing a "translate-in" to turn Kim Stafford's peace poem into as many languages as possible, I enthusiastically signed up. It turns out I was the only participant translating into French, but hearing other translators' versions in languages I could understand helped me improve my initial version, as did the conversation with Kim Stafford himself (how often do you get the fantastic opportunity to discuss with the author of a text you are asked to translate?).

I chose to adapt the title a bit by using the word *déclaration* in French instead of *proclamation*, which would have been a direct translation of the English, to both evoke and counterbalance the expression *déclaration de guerre* (declaration of war), which is a much more common phrase than its opposite *déclaration de paix* (declaration of peace). The biggest challenge for me was to find a way to render the "whereas," which is used no fewer than eight times in the poem. First, it is clearly a legal term frequently used in contracts, and legal documents are texts that make me break out in hives and that I never accept to translate. Second, according to the *Journal des traducteurs,* "The French culture...has a special, well-known aversion for repetition, not only of the same words but also of words of the same origin or root." I chose *étant donné que* rather than the legal phrase *attendu que*, which I just couldn't resort to, and used it only three times, replacing it by a simple *que* preceded by a comma in all other occurrences.

A note on Gaeilge by Sinéad Quirke Køngerskov
Compared to English, the syntax of the Irish language differs greatly. There is, for instance, much more inversion. For this poem, this means that many sentences read "the other way around" in Gaeilge: "a house on fire is the world," "small is hope," and "but true is war." The proclamation becomes more "poetic" in Irish. In Irish, the poet is not "afraid," rather he "has fear upon him." By traveling, the poems grows stronger.

Note, too, that in English the poem uses the "positive" form of all the verb tenses. It was not possible to transfer this to the Irish version because of how Irish works. "Whereas words are all I have" becomes "Whereas not do nothing have I but words."

Likewise, the verb "to be" has two forms in Irish—one that works relatively similarly to "to be" in English, and one that uses the verb "to do" as a kind of auxiliary verb. Thus, "Whereas kindness is seldom in the news" becomes "Whereas kindness does not be."

And whereas I was able to emulate the original version's economy of words in the Danish translation, I could not transfer that to the Gaeilge.

A note on German by Malcolm Goldman
What a wonderful poem to connect with! The first guiding principle for me in translating this poem was handling the meaning of the word "proclamation." This word can be translated into German in several ways, such as *Proklamation* or *Erlass*. *Erlass* is a more direct translation, however, while many English-language proclamations have positive connotations, the most well-known *Erlasse* in German history were used to subjugate and oppress. Yet *Proklamation* is most often used in a religious context. I felt that it more vividly reflects the mood of the poem—asserting a moral position and uplifting in the wake of its sorrow.

Following from this tonal decision, I branched away from the "whereas" structuring of the original poem, as this form is absent in both German legal proclamations and spiritual declarations. Here, I strove to match tonality: beginning with *während* (while) to situate the world in which the speaker finds themselves and then repeating "ei" sounds to evoke the lilting momentum of the original text. Subsequently, the English text picks up speed, with shorter elaborations of the state of the speaker's mind. Here I felt that the succinct, declarative assertions in German further contributed to the sense of urgency before the poem's final release. And how delighted I was to find that the English so seamlessly lent itself to German worldplay at the end with *Ruf* (calling) and *Beruf* (vocation) mirroring each other so serendipitously, just as the poem's hope breaks through the world's clouds. Thank you to Kim Stafford for writing such a beautiful piece.

A note on Greek by Konstantina Velisari
Though I don't usually work as a translator, I do like to learn different languages because we can discover interesting things from other cultures. The previous translation I did was for a scientific book in my field, and that was a completely different experience. This translation process has been very moving and emotional for me, because this poem addresses a very important and difficult issue impacting our world today.

Nowadays, war has become something very familiar for all of us. We read in the news about war in different parts of the world, while right next to that article we find advertisements for our favorite shampoo. This is completely absurd, and it is our responsibility to take a stand against war crimes. Art and poetry should be our inspiration and give us strength to fight for peace: for us, for our children, for all the children around the world.

A note on Hebrew by the editors
Hebrew is a member of the Canaanite group of Semitic languages. It was the language of the early Jews, but from around 586 BCE was replaced by Aramaic. By 200 CE use of Hebrew as an everyday language had largely

ceased, but it continued to be used for literary and religious functions, as well as a lingua franca among Jews from different countries. During the mid-19th century, efforts were made to revive Hebrew as an everyday language. Today it is spoken by about 5 million people, mainly in Israel, where it is an official language along with Arabic. A further 2 million people speak the language in other parts of the world.

Hebrew is written right to left in horizontal lines with the Hebrew alphabet, also known as the Hebrew Square Script, the square script, the block script, the Jewish script, or Ktav Ashuri.

A note on Hungarian by Erika Kóródi
While working on the translation, I stumbled upon a choral piece titled "Be It Therefore Resolved" by composer Joan Szymko, performed by the Aurora Chorus. This outstanding musical interpretation of Kim Stafford's "Proclamation for Peace" served as a source of inspiration and provided me with additional insight.

I would like to thank my friends and colleagues, Viktória Lebovics and Etelka Tamás-Balha for their thoughtful advice and valuable feedback on my translation.

A note on Icelandic by Kári Tulinius
This poem was difficult to render into Icelandic, because parliamentary proclamations in Iceland have no special

formulaic phrases, and never have. So I had to approximate the declarative power of the original language through other means, in this case by opting for more formal word choices when possible.

<u>A note on Italian by Marella Feltrin-Morris</u>
Translation is about making peace—not just with loss (that goes without saying), but with all the choices we discarded, all the versions we could have gone with, but didn't. And yet, when we're afforded the luxury of a translator's note, we often don't bother to make peace with them, do we? On the contrary, we treat each of those provisional choices as some sort of lame or even dangerous playmate, like Pinocchio's Lampwick, someone we shouldn't have listened to in the first place, but since we did, at least for a while, we now want to set the record straight and make sure everyone knows we no longer associate with them, and have moved on to worthier circles.

Given that Kim Stafford's poem is about peace, however, in reminiscing about my journey translating it, I would instead like to picture those discarded choices as welcome, albeit temporary, travel companions, whose voices I can still hear with gratitude, though we have since parted ways. *Premesso* is one of them: loud and a bit condescending, it took its seat claiming to be an appropriately bureaucratic equivalent of "whereas," flaunting its own succinctness and no-nonsense attitude.

When it saw me growing increasingly fond of the more discreet, gently-rolling *considerato,* it left on its own, before I had a chance to thank it for carrying the poem along during several drafts. *Minima* and *piccola* kept pushing each other off the wagon as translations of "small": the former accused the latter of not being dressed up enough for the occasion; the latter, unapologetic in its homeliness, insisted on showing its valid ticket as proof that it had every right to be there. When I called its bluff, *minima* good-naturedly withdrew its claim to a seat and wandered off. *Piccola,* on the other hand, still hasn't forgiven me for leaving it behind and continuing on with *poca cosa,* a couple of buddies that get along well with each other, but that haven't fully replaced the earnestness of *piccola.*

I wish to thank Kim Stafford for his encouragement to let his poem go where the sounds of our languages suggested. His trust in our instincts was both humbling and liberating. My gratitude also goes out to the brilliant and indefatigable Allison deFreese for conceiving this project and patiently carrying it to fruition, and to my niece Dora, whose keen Italian ear often guided me when I found myself at a crossroads.

A note on Japanese (I) by Mika Shimizu Jarmusz
Meeting Kim Stafford on Zoom with other translators to discuss this poem was the spark and catalyst for this translation. This Japanese version evolved through many

iterations, each different, over several months. With words carrying multiple meanings, diving through the depths of nuances in the source words to find the matching vivid imagery in the target phrasing was not straightforward. Simple phrases such as "house on fire," "all I have," and "I am free" presented the most difficulties. Japanese onomatopoeia and pillow words came in handy. A pillow word, 久方の (far and long before), which associates with "heaven, sky, rain, deity, light," paired nicely with "my calling—a song" without explicitly using those counterparts. Plain daily words are used in combination to render the "peaceful words" without using 平和 (peace), the go-to loan word cliché which always sounded abstract to my ear.

A note on Japanese (II) by Liu Jionghao
In Japanese, different sentence-ending patterns are used to convey various tones or attitudes. I have adopted the である format in this translation, which is commonly seen in formal documents, to echo the solemn attitude of this poem as a proclamation. Additionally, I believe a highlight of this translation lies in the use of the word 志事 (*shigoto*) in the last line. This word is pronounced the same as 仕事 (*shigoto*) which is more commonly used in everyday Japanese and means "work" or "occupation." On the other hand, 志事 is more formal and carries the meaning of "goal"

or "ambition." Through the homophonic nature of the characters, I have incorporated both the meanings of vocation and work into a single word.

A note on Kiswahili by the editors

Dunia is from Uganda and lives in a refugee camp in Zimbabwe. He has been an interpreter for the U.N. Last year, Dunia spoke from the camp in Zimbabwe at OSTI's 10th annual conference about the situation of refugees in Africa.

Kiswahili is a Bantu language of the Niger-Congo family and has a typical, complicated Bantu structure. The language shows influences from a variety of other languages, including Arabic, Portuguese, and German.

A note on Kurdish by the editors

Kurdish is a member of the Western Iranian branch of Indo-European languages. It is spoken by 20-40 million people in parts of Iraq, Turkey, Iran, Syria, Lebanon, Armenia, Georgia, Kyrgyzstan, Azerbaijan, Kazakhstan, and Afghanistan.

There are several dialects of Kurdish, including Northern Kurdish (Kurmanji), Central Kurdish (Soranî), and Southern Kurdish (Pehlewani). The dialects are not mutually intelligible.

A note on Latin by the editors

In the 5th century BCE, Latin was just one of many

languages spoken in central Italy. It was the language of Latium (modern Lazio), and Rome was a town of Latium. The earliest known inscriptions in Latin date from the 6th century BCE. The earliest surviving examples of Latin literature are Latin translations of Greek plays, and Cato's farming manual, which dates from 150 BCE.

As Rome expanded its influence over Italy and then other parts of Europe, North Africa, and the Middle East, it spread the language, too. Latin was used throughout the empire as the language of law and administration, and increasingly as the language of everyday life. Literacy was common among Roman citizens and the works of great Latin authors were read by many.

During the 15th century, Latin lost its dominant position as the main language of scholarship and religion throughout Europe. Latin remains in wide use today in the sciences and in law.

A note on Mandarin by Liu Jionghao
In Chinese, couplets often convey rhythm and emotional emphasis. Hence, I've included a pair of couplets at the beginning and end of the translation: they have equal word counts, and the components of the words correspond or are similar to each other, with meanings of words in the same position being more related to each other. Besides, in Chinese language, the use of the verb

"to be" is not as frequent and flexible as in English. Therefore, compared to the original poem, I have used more verbs than "is" or "are," making the translated poem more concrete and less abstract. For example, I translated "war is real" as 战争已在身边 (war surrounds us).

Another example is translating "a song not yet made shall be vocation and peaceful words the work of my remaining days" into a pair of couplets with verbs: 未来的诗歌，将承载我的宿命 (My future poetry will carry my destiny) and 和平的话语,将拥有我的余生 (The words of peace will possess my remaining years).

<u>A note on Nepali by the editors</u>
Nepali is a member of the Eastern Pahari branch of the Indo-Aryan language family spoken mainly in Nepal and northern India by about 25 million people. It is the primary language of Nepal's government, education, and the law. Historically, Nepali was called Khas Kura as spoken by the Khas people of Karnali, and Gorkhali as spoken by the people of the Gorkha Kingdom. Modern Nepali is believed to stem from Sinja Valley in Jumla.

Nepali was first written in the Brahmi script in about 980 CE during the reign of King Bhupal Damupal. From the 12th century, the Devanagari alphabet, which developed from the Brahmi script in the 11th century, became the primary script.

A note on Newar by the editors
Newar is a member of the Central Himalayan branch of the Tibeto-Burman language family. It is spoken mainly in the Kathmandu Valley of Nepal. In 2011, there were about 879,600 speakers of Newar in Nepal and about 14,000 speakers of Newar in northern India, as well as a few in Khasa (Dram/ Zhangmu) a town in Tibet on the border with Nepal.

Newar is also known as Newari, Nepal Bhasa, Newa Bhaye, Newaah Bhaae, Newaah Bhaaye, Newah, and Newal Bhaye. In Nepal it is taught in schools, used in the media and literature, and has official status in Kathmandu Metropolitan City.

Texts written in Newar emerged as early as the 12th century, written on palm-leaf manuscripts in the Nepal Lipi script, with Newar becoming an administrative language by the 14th century. The use of Newar has, at times, been officially censured in Nepal, with those who wrote or published in the language risking imprisonment. After 1990, the use of Newar in literature, schools, and the media began to increase again.

A note on Norwegian by the editors
Norwegian has around 5 million speakers primarily in Norway, with some speakers in Denmark, Sweden, Germany, the UK, Spain, Canada, and the U.S. In the , Norway was under Danish rule from roughly the 14th century until 1814, which impacted the Norwegian

language. Norwegian was spoken but Danish was used for official purposes, as a literary language, and in higher education.

After Norway separated from Denmark in 1814, Danish continued to be used in education until the 1830s, when a movement to create a new national language arose. The belief was that written Danish differed so much from spoken Norwegian it was difficult to learn and that every country should have its own language.

From this, two languages emerged: Landsmål (a national language, renamed Nynorsk in 1929), which was based on colloquial Norwegian and regional dialects, and and Riksmål (officially known as Bokmål), used primarily as a written language, and quite similar to Danish.

Nowadays schools in Norway teach both variations of the language. Students learn both and then choose which one they would like to learn as a major language. Civil servants are expected to be able to use both.

The Scandinavian languages of Norway, Denmark, and Sweden are mutually intelligible.

A note on Pashto by the editors
Pashto is an Indo-Iranian language spoken in Afghanistan, Pakistan, and Iran. There are also Pashto speakers in Tajikistan and India, as well as the UAE and Saudi Arabia.

There are three main varieties of Pashto: Northern Pashto, spoken mainly in northern Pakistan; Southern Pashto, spoken mainly in Afghanistan; and Central Pashto, also spoken mainly in Pakistan. The exact number of Pashto speakers is not known with certainty but the estimate is 45 million to 55 million speakers.

Pashto was first written down in the 16th century with a version of Arabic script. There are two standard written forms, based on the Kandahar and the Peshawar dialects. Pashto was made the national language of Afghanistan by royal decree in 1936.

A note on Persian by the editors
A Western Iranian language, Persian is spoken by about 130 million people, mainly in Iran, Afghanistan, and Tajikistan, as well as in Uzbekistan, Iraq, Russia, and Azerbaijan. There are about 72 million native speakers of Persian, and about 38 million second-language speakers. Persian was the language of government in Turkey, central Asia, and India for centuries, and until 1900 in Kashmir.

Old Persian was first written about 600 BCE with a Cuneiform script. After the Islamic conquest of the Persian Sassanian Empire in the 7th and 8th centuries CE, the Arabic alphabet was adapted to write the Persian language. This is now known as the Persian or Perso-Arabic alphabet and is written right to left in horizontal lines with numerals written left to right.

<u>A note on Polish by the editors</u>
Polish is a West Slavonic language spoken mainly in Poland. About 40 million people speak Polish world wide. As a language, Polish is closely related to Kashubian, Sorbian, Czech, and Slovak.

Polish first appeared in writing in 1136 in the "Gniezno papal bull" (Bulla gnieźnieńska), which included 410 Polish names. The first written Polish sentence was *day ut ia pobrusa a ti poziwai* (I'll grind [the corn] in the quern and you'll rest), which appeared in *Ksiega henrykowska* in 1270.

The most famous writer of Polish origin is perhaps Joseph Conrad or Konrad Korzeniowski (1857–1924), who wrote in English and authored, among many novels, *Heart of Darkness*.

<u>A note on Portuguese by the editors</u>
Portuguese is a Romance language spoken by about 255 million people. It is the official language of Portugal, Brazil, Cape Verde, Guinea-Bissau, Angola, São Tomé, Mozambique, and Príncipe, and is also an official language in East Timor, Equatorial Guinea, and Macau.

Portuguese comes from Latin, brought to the Iberian Peninsula by Roman soldiers, settlers, and merchants, where the language was influenced by the Hispano-Celtic languages spoken there at the time.

The earliest records of a distinctly Portuguese language appear in documents dating from the 9th century CE from the kingdom of Galicia, which corresponds to modern Galicia in Spain, and part of northern Portugal. From the 15th century, the Portuguese began to colonize parts of Africa, Asia, and the Americas (including the region known today as Brazil), taking their language with them.

A note on Punjabi by Moazzam Sheikh
My co-translator Amna Ali and I had fun translating the poem into Punjabi, both for preserving the sense of the original and the challenge to render the beauty and rhythm of the English poem into a modern day Punjabi as poetically as possible.

A note on Quechua by Guipsy Alata Ramos
Many thoughts surfaced for me as I translated this poem, some personal and others related to either national or international social contexts. Given that we are experiencing a very difficult time at a global level, to reflect on the meaning of peace, freedom, and on our role in the world is quite complex. As I translated this poem, I also thought about the paths that each one of us travels in our life, and of our moments of struggle when faced with challenges that may arise.

On the other hand, I thought what a wonderful opportunity this would be to communicate these issues in my native language, so my language might be seen and read by people who are curious about it. I hoped this would be an opportunity for such readers to discover the diversity of our visions and languages as we communicate for literary content, as well as intersective thoughts that inspire us deeply, and in a way that allows us to so enrich those around us.

A note on Romani by the editors

Romani is an Indo-Aryan language spoken by about five to six million Roma people throughout Europe and the U.S. The largest concentrations of Roma people live in Turkey, Spain, and Romania.

Although Romani is mainly an oral language, it is written primarily in the Latin alphabet, and to some extent in the Greek, Cyrillic, Arabic, and Devanagari alphabets. Romani was first written during the 16th century, when glossaries were produced by non-Romani scholars. This translation is in the Romani language as spoken in Poland, and so will include Polish loan words.

A note on Romanian by Ileana Marin

At first sight, Kim Stafford's lines seemed easy to translate as they record a reality of which we are all too aware. Once I started penning my translation, then typing the multiple variants of the direct, honest, and bold simplicity of the poem, I realized the difficulty: the perspicuity of a crystal-clear expression of urgency. Hard choices among the Romanian versions of the poem crowded my desk. The breakthrough came when I read the poem out loud and heard myself uttering the list of empirical facts that characterize the turmoil of the contemporary world. Suddenly, I recalled Wittgenstein's adage from *Tractatus Logico-Philosophicus* that "The world is the totality of facts, not of things." It became clear that I had to focus on the straightforward expression of the factual information in order to do justice to Kim Stafford's "A Proclamation for Peace." Facts result from actions or lack of actions; to change the facts, the poet takes action through his poetry, the only authentic way for a poet. The poem is, in the end, a new fact that was added to the world. Yet, through translation, that single fact is multiplied exponentially. I feel that through my translation I am contributing to the circulation of the poem, which may result in a much more impactful fact. Kim Stafford's calling has been heard and his vocation has been embraced by me and all the other translators in this volume.

A note on Russian by Gleb & Vita Sapozhnikov
Translating "A Proclamation for Peace" posed unique challenges, the main one being the phenomenon of a proclamation itself (the flow of multiple *Whereas* clauses culminating in a *Therefore* conclusion), which is an English-language form not practiced in Russian culture. The translator must look at the closest resembling Russian artifacts, which were the tsars'

manifestos and Lenin's decrees. Reviewing these materials helped form a common theme that brought structure to the translation with repetitive use of a somewhat archaic Russian equivalent of "whereas," which called for an archaic "therefore," and evoked the tsarist manifestos in the translation of the title.

Another challenge was to translate the second line, where I originally equated "shouting" to **вопль**. Vita, ever attuned to the language, called me on that: "shouting" is in fact **крик**, while **вопль** is "shriek" or "cry" and her remark made me truly understand what the second line is about—in the poet's mind the nations are arguing, with a sea of shouting from everybody at everybody else. We corrected the line to reflect this.

It is worth mentioning a lesser issue with the last line, which I originally translated **отведённых мне дней** because it sounded nice, but Vita is a demanding editor and told me the meaning deviates: **отведённых мне** means "measured out for me," not quite "my remaining." I went with a more mundane-sounding, but true-to-the-original, **оставшихся мне дней**.

A note on Spanish (Latin American) by Romina Espinosa

The translation for this poem was a delightful creative process. I did not want to just do a translation. This is *different*. This is art. We are talking about poetry! I wanted to make a transcreation, something melodic where words resonate with the soul. Our ancestors from time immemorial told us oral stories. Literature, poetry, goes beyond the written tradition as we know it in Western cultures. While keeping this idea in mind as a woman with ancestral Peruvian roots, I utilized various online resources, including listening to Latin American folk songs and recalling lessons learned in my Spanish choir singing class. I looked for sensory words and rhythm where Spanish listeners from Northern Mexico through Colombia's Tayrona, Peru's Andes Mountains to Argentina's Patagonia could connect with all five senses. This translation taught me that various factors are taken into account when translating a poem. It goes beyond making an accurate word selection. I was able to reflect on the sociocultural and linguistic complexity in Latin America's modern times. There are many diverse identities within Latin American countries. This translation is my love rendition for the land, the people, and the Spanish language. My hope is to see peace in this region of the world and beyond. *Paz.*

A note on Swedish by the editors
Swedish is spoken by about 10 million people worldwide. It is also the official second language of Finland and is the fourth most spoken Germanic language.

Early Old Swedish (klassisk fornsvenska or äldre

fornsvenska) first appeared in the Latin alphabet in 1225 in the Westrogothic Law (Äldre Västgötalagen), the law code law used in West Gotland. Between 1375 and 1526, the language of Sweden was known as Late Old Swedish (yngre fornsvenska). The translation of the Bible into Swedish in 1526 is seen as marking the emergence of modern Swedish.

Modern Swedish spelling rules were created by the author Carl Gustaf af Leopold, who was commissioned by the Swedish Academy (Svenska Akademien). His proposal was published in 1801, and finally adopted by the Academy in 1874. Swedish spelling was reformed in 1906, and that reform was not supported by the Swedish Academy until 1950.

A note on Tagalog by the editors

Tagalog is a language of the Central Philippine branch of the Austronesian (Malay Polynesian) family.

Tagalog speakers are also found in Canada, Guam, the Midway Islands, Saudi Arabia, the UAE, the UK, and the U.S. The roughly 14 million native Tagalog speakers form the second largest linguistic and cultural group in the Philippines.

Tagalog derives from *tagá-ílog*, which means "resident beside the river." Little is known of the history of the language before the arrival of the Spanish in the Philippines during the 16th century as no earlier written sources have yet been found.

The earliest known book in Tagalog is the *Doctrina Cristiana* (*Christian Doctrine*) which was published in 1593. It was written in Spanish and Tagalog, with the Tagalog text in both Baybayin and the Latin alphabet. Tagalog was written with the Baybayin script until the 17th century, after which the Latin alphabet was used. Today the Baybayin script is used primarily for decorative purposes.

The national language of the Philippines, known as Filipino (Wikang Filipino), is a standard register of Tagalog and is defined by the Commission on the Filipino Language (Komisyon sa Wikang Filipino) as "the native language, spoken and written, in Metro Manila, the National Capital Region, and in other urban centers of the archipelago."

A note on Tamil by the editors
Tamil is an ancient Dravidian language spoken today by around 68 million people in regions of Southeast Asia including Tamil Nadu (where it is the official language of this southern India state), Sri Lanka, and Singapore.

A note on Thai by Piyawee Ruenjinda
Kim's "A Proclamation for Peace" resonated deeply with me. As I read, I felt a profound sense of urgency and the severity of the challenges we face, accompanied by feelings of isolation and almost helplessness. The poem seemed to harness these emotions to create something—

a song—intended to bring peace to humanity. I
endeavored to maintain the same tone in the Thai
translation as in the original poem. I also found it
intriguing to compare my interpretation with that of my
counterpart Chintana Barden. Many thanks to Allison
for initiating this project and to Chintana for involving
me in it. For Peace!

A note on Ukrainian by Ilana Ianofska
I used to believe in the power of words, until my home
was attacked by russia. Experiencing tragedy on this
scale, words lost their meaning to me. Working on the
poem reminded me of my values and of the fact that,
although language may not be the most powerful
weapon, it is the best I, as a civilian, have.

A note on Upper Austrian by Carola F. Berger
I decided to try my hand at translating Kim Stafford's
"A Proclamation for Peace" into Upper Austrian, which
belongs to the Bavarian language family. More
specifically, it is classified as a Central Bavarian dialect,
which in turn is a variant of German. Opinions vary as
to whether Bavarian should be considered as a language
separate from German, or as a variant.

Further, Bavarian spoken in Bavaria (a part of
Germany) differs from the dialects classified as
Bavarian that are spoken in Austria. I grew up in Upper
Austria, and while everyone speaks some dialect in

Austria, the written language is "proper" German, with a few Austrian idiosyncrasies.

I usually translate highly-technical texts into and from German and therefore, poetry has been quite the change for me, Upper Austrian seemed easier than "proper" German. However, my initial attempts failed, and things only started flowing when I deviated from Kim Stafford's original format and started rhyming, while adhering to the proclamation format and the content of the original as closely as possible.

The second hurdle was writing things down, because, as mentioned above, I learned how to write "proper" German in school, but not dialect. For example, some vowels differ significantly from their pronunciation in German. To solve this, I decided to spell things in accordance with Wikipedia articles on Bavarian spelling, but also to produce a voice recording for folks who are unsure of the correct Upper Austrian pronunciation.

A note on Vietnamese by Tram Bui & Hai Tran
Tram: She felt a strong personal connection while transcreating this poem because she, too, is a refugee of the Vietnam War. The poem spoke to her as a plea for peace in this volatile world we now live in. She identifies herself as the "single bird on a wire," using her skills as an interpreter and translator to be the "vocation" of her "remaining days." She and Mr. Hai Tran, her Vietnamese co-transcreator, took into consideration the

tone, rhythm and melody of poetry, all the while paying respect to the poet's intentions. The culture of the Vietnamese people, and the language nuances of her beloved Vietnamese, were also factors in how the poem was transcreated during the collaboration. She feels blessed and honored to have a small part in this translation and transcreation project. Thank you to Kim Stafford, the author, for this beautiful poem, and thank you to Allison deFreese for choosing her and Mr. Hai Tran to transcreate this poem, "A Plea for Peace," for the Vietnamese people. In the end, we only have our words to plead for peace and kindness.

Hai: Regarding the poem "A Proclamation for Peace," he understands that the author, Kim Stafford, is hurt by wars. Two examples are the devastating war between Russia and Ukraine and the Israel and Palestine war in Gaza. According to Hai's interpretation, Kim Stafford feels like he is a victim of the wars. Kim has lost everything, except for his words. Thus, he would like to use his words and this poem to plead for a peaceful world.

A note on Yoruba by Abayo Animashaun

Yoruba is an old language that's rich in idiom. And even though I've spoken it all my life, my proficiencies within it are limited. Thus, this version of Kim Stafford's "A Proclamation for Peace" is more a free verse equivalent than an exact literary translation.

<u>A note on Yucatec Maya by the editors</u>
Yucatec Maya is among the most widely spoken of the some 30 Mayan languages used in Mesoamerica today, with around 800,000 speakers in Mexico's Yucatan Peninsula, Belize, and northern Guatemala. One of the challenges of translating this poem into Yucatec Maya was in rendering concepts that were not originally part of Mayan language or culture. The word "wire," for example, which is commonplace in English, required a Spanish loan word (*cable*) in this Yucatec Maya translation.

<u>A note on Zapotec by Paul E. Riek</u>
There are many versions of the Zapotec language. Isthmus Zapotec is spoken in the "Isthmus," the southeastern part of the state of Oaxaca. Juchitan is the largest city in that region. Unlike other versions of the language, much literature has been published in Isthmus Zapotec.

<u>A note on the recordings by the editors</u>
Scanning the QR codes with a phone, readers should be able to hear many of the translations voiced. Most of the recordings were made in informal settings, and audio clarity varies—you can sometimes catch sounds from the street behind the voice. But you will hear the expressive heart of the poem traveling through these voices unencumbered by distinctions of place or language. It may be here this book most comes to life.

<u>A note on the double translations</u>
When we started this project, two Japanese translators responded immediately, so we decided to honor their generous enthusiasm by including both.

With the Spanish, again we had two volunteers, and since the Spanish language is often distinctive in Central and South America, we have included both the "world Spanish" of D.P. Snyder, and the Latin American Spanish of Romina Espinosa.

<u>A note on the cover photograph by the editors</u>
Michael Nye took the photo of a Palestinian child in the village of Jalizone in 1988. The girl is holding a poem by Mahmoud Darwish. Here is an excerpt translated by Aziz Shihab:

> I long for my mother's bread
> And my mother's coffee
> And my mother's touch
> And my childhood grows up
> One day following days full of patience
> And I love my life
> Because if I die
> My mother's tears will shame me